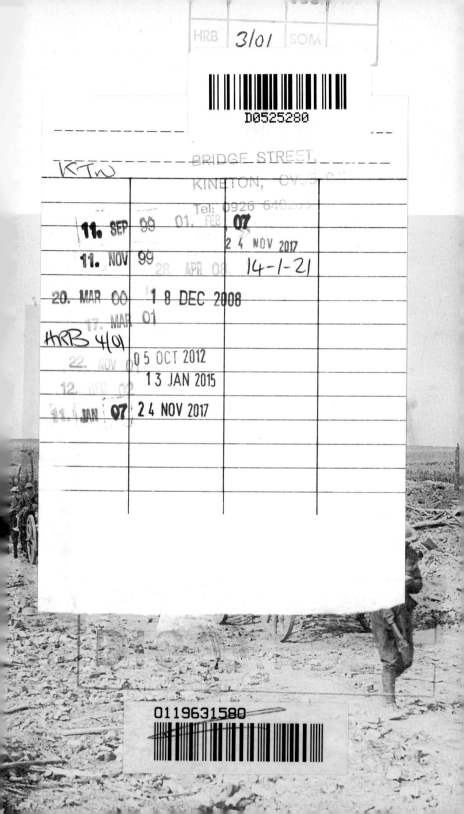

Other guides in the Battleground Europe Series:

Walking the Salient *by* Paul Reed
Ypres - Sanctuary Wood and Hooge *by* Nigel Cave
Ypres - Hill 60 *by* Nigel Cave
Ypres - Messines Ridge *by* Peter Oldham

Walking the Somme *by* Paul Reed
Somme - Gommecourt *by* Nigel Cave
Somme - Serre *by* Jack Horsfall & Nigel Cave
Somme - Beaumont Hamel *by* Nigel Cave
Somme - Thiepval *by* Michael Stedman
Somme - La Boisselle *by* Michael Stedman
Somme - Fricourt *by* Michael Stedman
Somme - Carnoy-Montauban *by* Graham Maddocks
Somme - Pozieres *by* Graham Keech
Somme - Courcelette *by* Paul Reed
Somme - Boom Ravine *by* Trevor Pidgeon
Somme - Mametz Wood *by* Michael Renshaw
Somme - Advance to Victory (North) 1918 *by* Michael Stedman

Arras - Vimy Ridge *by* Nigel Cave
Arras - Bullecourt *by* Graham Keech

Hindenburg Line *by* Peter Oldham
Epehy *by* Bill Mitchenson
Riqueval *by* Bill Mitchenson

Boer War - The Relief of Ladysmith, Colenso, Spion Kop *by* Lewis Childs

Accrington Pals Trail *by* WilliamTurner

Poets at War: Wilfred Owen *by* Helen McPhail and Philip Guest

Gallipoli *by* Nigel Steel

Battleground Europe Series guides in preparation:

Ypres - Polygon Wood *by* Nigel Cave
La Bassée - Givenchy *by* Michael Orr
La Bassée - Neuve Chapelle 1915 *by* Geoff Bridger
Walking Arras *by* Paul Reed
Arras - Monchy le Preux *by* Colin Fox
Somme - Following the Ancre *by* Michael Stedman
Somme - High Wood *by* Terry Carter
Somme - Advance to Victory 1918 *by* Michael Stedman
Somme - Ginchy *by* Michael Stedman
Somme - Combles *by* Paul Reed
Somme - Beaucourt *by* Michael Renshaw

Walking Verdun *by* Paul Reed

Poets at War: Edmund Blunden *by* Helen McPhail and Philip Guest

Boer War - The Siege of Ladysmith *by* Lewis Childs
Isandhlwana *by* Ian Knight and Ian Castle
Rorkes Drift *by* Ian Knight and Ian Castle

With the continued expansion of the Battleground series a Battleground Europe Club has been formed to benefit the reader. The purpose of the Club is to keep members informed of new titles and key developments by way of a quarterly newsletter, and to offer many other reader-benefits. Membership is free and by registering an interest you can help us predict print runs and thus maintain prices at their present levels. Please call the office 01226 734555, or send your name and address along with a request for more information to:

Battleground Europe Club
Pen & Sword Books Ltd, 47 Church Street, Barnsley, South Yorkshire S70 2AS

Battleground Europe

DELVILLE WOOD

NIGEL CAVE

Series editor
Nigel Cave

LEO COOPER

This book is dedicated to Janet and Tom Fairgrieve. Over the years they have welcomed thousands of people to the South African Memorial and willingly shared of their time, expertise and friendship. They have contributed much to ensuring that younger generations *Remember.*

First published in 1999 by
LEO COOPER
an imprint of
Pen Sword Books Limited
47 Church Street, Barnsley, South Yorkshire S70 2AS

ISBN 0 85052 584 5

A CIP catalogue of this book is available
from the British Library

Printed by St Edmundsbury Press Limited
Bury St Edmunds, Suffolk

*For up-to-date information on other titles produced under the Leo Cooper imprint,
please telephone or write to:*
Pen & Sword Books Ltd, FREEPOST, 47 Church Street
Barnsley, South Yorkshire S70 2AS
Telephone 01226 734222

CONTENTS

**A working party carrying duckboards through
Longueval in September 1916.**

INTRODUCTION

Delville Wood is one of those places on the Somme to which almost every battlefield tour or visitor will go. This is generally the case for even regular visitors to the Somme. To be honest, what often attracts them are the comfortable facilities in the Visitors' Centre, the chance to make a comfortable lavatory stop, to sit at bench picnic tables and enjoy a bite to eat, to peruse the excellent collection of books for sale, drink a coffee or just chat. Battlefield touring is not all leaping around clutching maps!

This scene is such a wild contrast to the events of so many years ago, when men were dying in agony, the air rent with shell bursts, bodies bursting from their uniforms in the scorching heat of July and August 1916, the whole atmosphere overpowering in its stench of gas and decomposition, filled with the smoke from shell bursts and the dust from the parched earth and tracks.

How dare we carry on such banal and trivial tasks in such a place?

I have no problem with this dichotomy. The purpose of the South Africans in obtaining Delville Wood after the war was to serve as a permanent tribute to what their men achieved on the Western Front during the Great War and this has been extended, in the shape of the beautifully designed and executed Museum – to the Second World War. Would people be aware of South Africa's contributions if the Visitors' Centre and Museum did not exist? Would so many people be coming here if it were not so comfortable for the visitor? The answer is that they certainly would not, and so what has been achieved is to make people aware of this past. Recent developments have also enabled the role of those who served in the war who were coloured and black to be made known. And perhaps more people than just myself ponder this contrast and also think more deeply about the issues that this raises about the cost and purpose of war, about the destructive nature of warfare, about the two extremes of human nature, the destructive and hateful and the sacrificial and courageous. In all, I think the South African Memorial at Delville Wood serves a far greater purpose than the utilitarian.

When I first came to Delville Wood in the summer of 1968 there might have been about two thousand visitors during the year. For every visitor then there is probably about thirty now, many of who are school children from the United Kingdom. Yet although numbers have increased so tremendously, Delville Wood is generally a quiet place: it is, after all, a vast wooded expanse, the only one of the great woods of

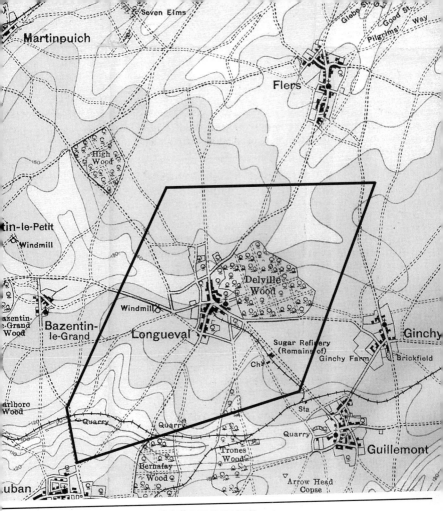

LIST OF MAPS

the Somme battlefield open to public access. Visitors often do not explore very much of this wood; they park at the Visitors' Centre, they go to the Museum, walking up the impressive approach, they come back for a coffee and they go. To be fair, this is all that a packed schedule will often allow. On the other hand it is a place that invites a reflective walk amongst beautiful, mature trees with the evidence of ravaged ground visible off the rides. This is hallowed ground, a war grave. It witnessed such a variety of human emotions in the six or seven weeks that battle raged here so fiercely.

It was here that my grandfather came the closest to death during the conflict, when a shell landed at his feet, splashing him with mud all over; it was a blind, and failed to detonate. He was en route to the line at Flers and Guedecourt, to his battalion, the 7th Leicesters, bringing up the rations in his task as a CQMS. It is an important place for me.

Nigel Cave
Ely Place, London

The village of Longueval showing a street and stumps of Delville Wood. The photograph was taken in June 1917.

SITE OF CHATEAU

PRINCES STREET

ACKNOWLEDGEMENTS

As for so many of my other books in this series, my first acknowledgement must be to the authors of the Divisional and Regimental histories and of the various War Diaries from which the bulk of the writing is gleaned, and from which much is directly quoted. I am unapologetic about this for who best to describe what happened than people who were, more often than not in the case of this particular book, themselves present? Although the writers of the War Diaries were writing an official record to be used for a variety of purposes such as inquiries into a particular battle, a record for the Battalion and the use of historians (ie authorised military ones), this did not necessarily prevent at least some of them from writing movingly. Regimental and divisional histories can be a very mixed bag of records, but the 9th Division has been particularly well served by its historian, Major John Ewing, who successfully manages to describe so much of what he wrote with great verve as well as accuracy. He won the MC and a bar, serving in 6/KOSB.

For the German accounts I am once more indebted to my unseen, but good, friend, Ralph Whitehead. A very busy family man, he has still found time to spend hours churning out translations of German divisional and regimental records, and has thereby done all of us the great service of giving us a story as seen from the other side of the line. Too often the British have a tendency to see the war in isolation, and Ralph's work has enabled me to portray something of what the Germans underwent.

I am grateful to RHQ of the Royal Highlanders for assisting me with War Diary material, particularly that relating to the Seaforth Highlanders. Monsieur J Bommeleijn of Longueval welcomed me to his home and enabled me to obtain copies of a considerable number of his extensive postcard collection of Longueval before and during the war. His generosity has made a considerable contribution to the illustrations in this book.

Trips now to the Somme are not only a matter of visiting the battlefields and paying respects to those who were killed in the war in the beautifully maintained cemeteries so lovingly and carefully tended by the Commonwealth War Graves Commission, but also of seeing a growing circle of friends. In particular I would like to mention several by name. For all of my trips whilst working on this book I have stayed at the Bed and Breakfast run by Julie and Michael Renshaw, *Les Galets,* between Beaumont and Auchonvillers. A cheery welcome, plenty of good chat, excellent rooms and wonderful cooking – as well as being great friends; just what is required after a miserable, wet day on the battlefields.

For nearly all of the time that I have been coming to the Somme I have been aware of Tom and Janet Fairgrieve. In the early days it was because I saw Tom's name in the visitors' register in the Delville Wood group of cemeteries from his work as the Head Gardener. In more recent years it has been through their work at the South African Memorial, Tom as the custodian of the deeply impressive museum and Janet as the lady who oversees the best bookshop on the Somme, not to mention the ever-acceptable steaming hot cups of coffee. They have become firm friends over the years, and it is in the visitors' centre there that I have met so many others with a great interest in the war with a whole wealth of knowledge of their own. I am very grateful to Tom and Janet and for the work that they have done in keeping the memory of South Africa s contribution in the war alive, and so it is that I have dedicated this book to them.

As is usual on my visits others, who were touring with me, have willingly undertaken diversions to the Delville Wood area and to spend longer there than one might usually. My thanks go, therefore, to my father, Colonel Terry Cave and to Colonels Dick Burge and Terry Holloway; to a number of former pupils, Dan and James Saunders, Mark Fisher and Paul Spencer and to Professor Brian Bond and Dr George Bailey from the Department of War Studies at King's College, London. Particular thanks are due to Richard Brucciani for flying me over the Somme, giving both of his time and his aircraft.

The team at Pen and Sword books have remained as tolerant as ever (probably through gritted teeth) as they deal with late scripts and laughably inadequate sketch maps. Roni and Paul Wilkinson manage to make sense of it all, as ever, and do so with Yorkshire good humour.

The work of the Commonwealth War Graves Commission continues to be as impressive as ever. Over the last eighteen months or so I have seen, for example, the wonderful work done at Ovillers British Cemetery, which has involved the complete horticultural gutting of the cemetery and its re-emergence as a place of solemn beauty; a fitting place to hold the young men of so many years ago whose lives were lost in that Great War. The work is, by its nature, never ending, but it is most encouraging to see the vast increase over recent years of people who visit and can thus appreciate what is being done to perpetuate remembrance.

ADVICE TO TOURERS

Access from Calais to the battlefield from Calais is usually via the A26 and the A1 (Paris) autoroutes, exiting at Bapaume. Take the D29 to Albert (also signed Amiens) and follow this road until approaching the north east end of Courcelette, where there is a turning to the south east for Martinpuich, but is also signed 'South African Memorial'. This will lead you through the little village of Martinpuich, the road leading into this from the north known as Gun Pit Lane during the war, the scene of dreadful slaughter amongst the Germans in September 1916. Continue along this road (but beware of priority from the right at the crossroads in the centre of the village), which in due course brings you past High Wood, another of the great woods of the Somme over which fighting raged for many bloody weeks. To the south east may be seen the great mass of Delville Wood. At the road junction turn left (on your right you will see a wooden cross, commemorating 12/Glosters) which brings you almost immediately into Longueval, a typical Somme village of about 300 souls. At the cross roads in the centre of town proceed straight ahead and after a few hundred yards there is another turning to the left (the village cemetery is on the right of this road); two flagpoles, usually flying the South African and French flags, mark the entrance to the visitors' centre of the South African Memorial.

For touring purposes you will find the French IGN Green series most useful – in this case 4 Laon Arras. For the detailed work around Longueval and Delville Wood it would be most helpful to be equipped with the IGN Blue Series (1:25000). 2408 East (Bray-sur-Somme) covers the immediate area around Delville Wood, but it would also be useful to have 2407 East (Bapaume) which includes Flers, the main support position for the Germans. These maps are usually available in *Libraire* or *Maison de Presse*; there are a couple of these shops in the

Bapaume Street in Albert.

square in front of the basilica in Albert. There are also 1:250000 Michelin maps overprinted with the locations of Commonwealth War Graves cemeteries; these are sometimes available at Delville Wood or from the Maidenhead headquarters of the CWGC, whose details appear later in this section. The maps cost approximately £3. The interested might want to get the relevant trench maps; the best way of doing this is to become a member of the Western Front Association, which runs a trench map service (and from whom, incidentally, you may also purchase the above mentioned Blue IGN maps). The relevant trench map (1:10000) is sheet 57c SW 3 Longueval. The map corrected to 29.9.16 is the most useful in that most of the trenches are named; whilst that dated 31.7.16 shows the German front line on 14 July 1916. GH Smith & Son of York have reprinted a large range of trench maps at approximately 70% of the original size, but on good quality glossy paper and in colour at a competitive price. The full range is usually available at Delville Wood; the Longueval map reproduced by the company is that corrected to 15.8.16, which shows many of the trench lines, but these are unfortunately unlabelled.

A day can quite easily be spent touring this part of the Somme. A fuller appreciation of what was going on in this area prior to the attack on 14 July may be had from Mike Stedman's *Fricourt-Mametz* and Michael Renshaw's *Mametz Wood* in this series. The presence of the facilities at Delville Wood for purchasing books, maps and a variety of soft and hot drinks; good clean toilets and outside bench seating and tables make it an unusually convenient place for making a tour of a part of the battlefield. Visitors should be aware that the centre (as is the Museum) is shut on Mondays, for the winter months – ie December and January at the least, and for French national holidays. It is easy to purchase your picnic lunch in Albert   there is a supermarket on your left as one is approaching the centre of Albert, after the roundabout, from the direction of Bapaume. Whilst in there getting food and wine, also purchase a corkscrew and plastic mug or glasses. One may also obtain petrol here, and at the end of your touring there is a very handy car wash to enable you to rediscover the original colour of your car.

The country around here is generally rolling and open, but Caterpillar Valley, which runs between Montauban and Longueval, provides plenty of dead ground. The stream that formed it has long since disappeared. The walking is generally very easy, and stout walking boots should be quite sufficient for almost any weather conditions, certainly when the sane would be out for a walk! Although Delville Wood is never far away when following the tours, it is always a good idea to carry bottled water, as it can get very hot. Also in your knapsack you should carry (or would find useful) a pair of binoculars, a camera, a notebook to keep a record of the photographs taken (one field looks very much like another when back home!) and a compass.

The tracks around Delville Wood are all freely available to the public. However, this does not mean that they are also a car park: this is a working area, and the tracks are there for the convenience of the farmer. Please do not leave your vehicle blocking any of these routes; or at the very least do not wander away more than a few yards from them should you decide to stop and have a look around at some particular vantage point. Do not assume that you can walk over fields and into woods: no one objects immediately after the harvest, but the same rules apply in France as in Britain – if in doubt, ask permission and never walk over fields with crops in them. The woods are private and are maintained, amongst other things, for hunting. The autumn and early winter months are extremely dangerous on the Somme, especially on a Sunday morning, when everyone seems to turn out with a gun and dogs and to blaze away at anything that moves – and it could be you. Most definitely stay out of woods – or anywhere near them

This map gives the idea of the Longueval plateau and the rolling ground around it.

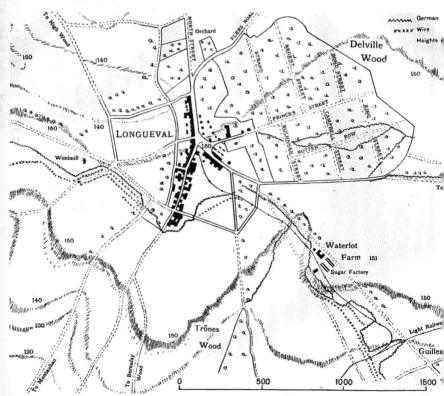

during this time. Fatalities are really quite common from hunting accidents.

Please do not bring a metal detector to the Somme; amongst other things it is quite illegal to use them on someone else's land. Even worse, do not set about digging. This has got to almost epidemic proportions and such activities have, understandably, infuriated local people. It makes it all the more difficult for those who simply wish to explore. People should be warned that it is an offence to dig up artefacts and that the law enables not only metal detectors to be confiscated but also the car. Representations are being made to the police to carry out the penalties prescribed.

This quite regrettable habit has even extended to within the boundaries of Delville Wood itself. This is reprehensible, not only for the reasons listed above, because the whole of Delville Wood is an official War Grave. Visitors are warned that it is potentially very hazardous to go off the clearly visible rides, trench and former railway lines within the wood. The area has never been fully cleared of ammunition and much of it remains close to, or on, the surface. Some idea of the extent of this may be appreciated from when the ground was cleared for the visitors' centre some fifteen years or so ago; literally tons of shells and hundreds of grenades had to be removed. Gas shells were used extensively during the battle of 1916 in the wood, and these are particularly dangerous munitions eighty years on, given their unusually thin skins. All munitions are potentially lethal and should be left alone. Safe

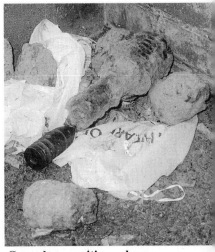

Grenades awaiting clearance – Delville Wood, summer 1998.

souvenirs may be purchased in the shop. There is a small deer herd in the wood, and this means that it is quite possible to pick up Lyme disease. This is caused by the bite of a tiny deer tick, which proceeds to burrow into you. the disease it causes can be dormant for years and then result in a whole galaxy of symptoms – not usually lethal, but certainly enough to make one wonder if life is worth living (actually, chronic depression is another result of this little bug's presence) ultimately resulting in incontinence and loss of mental faculties. The moral of all this is that one should keep out of the undergrowth. One might be wise to wear trousers and long-sleeve shirts, but on the other hand there is no point in getting paranoid!

Before going to the battlefields it is worth your while to make a visit to the National Army Museum and the Imperial War Museum. Both have interesting exhibits and displays and the IWM in particular has a very well stocked bookshop. Both these museums have reading rooms with an extensive library of regimental histories and personal recollections. An appointment is all that is required from the IWM; a Reader's Ticket for the NAM. In Albert there is an excellent and constantly expanding museum in the old air raid shelters under the town. Access is by the basilica, with the exit in the park. Further afield, and handy on a miserable day, is the *Historial* at Peronne, where a good half day can easily be spent looking at the great array of exhibits of weapons and uniforms, documents, newspapers and video clips.

Should you wish to trace a relative who served in the war there is a possibility that his or her papers might have survived the blitz and be available at the Public Record Office. There is an excellent publication published by that organisation, *Army Service Records of the First World War*. The PRO can appear a very daunting place, but the staff are uniformly (in my experience) helpful and willing to steer the dimmest of us through the various procedures.

If you are tracing someone who was killed, the CWGC can usually help you find the location of their commemoration or burial. The barest minimum is name and initial, but that might result in literally hundreds of possibilities, so regiment and battalion, number, date (at least approximately) of death and at least the country of death all combine to make the search that much easier. A charge may be levied, according to circumstances. The CWGC has its area office just on the outskirts of Arras, in Beaurains. They have a full record of casualties as well. The CWGC does an enormously impressive job, and it would be appreciated if you took the time to fill in the Visitors' Book which is found in all but the smallest cemeteries; in these seemingly perpetual times of financial stringency the number of recorded visitors adds to the CWGC cause when the time comes to plead for funding.

For your vehicle you should have the registration document and a copy of your insurance; a Green Card is not usually required now for France, but check with your insurers. A First Aid Kit, spare light bulbs and a warning triangle are all compulsory. The French police are quite keen on spot checks, so do not forget your driving licence either. It is probably worthwhile pointing out that French drink and driving laws are now stricter than those in the UK, so do not be heavy handed with the wine bottle at lunch time.

For yourself and your passengers I would strongly recommend full personal medical and health insurance; though the form E1 11, available from main post offices, does give reciprocal cover. This does not cover all costs, however, in France, and can leave you with a hefty bill to pay. Ensure that you take the standard medications with you, and given the amount of rusty iron lying around, a tetanus booster would be sensible.

Theft from cars is not unusual, so please follow the standard sensible precautions.

Accommodation can usually be had easily on the Somme, though the time immediately around 1 July is usually booked up early. There are also a large number of bed and breakfasts in the area, British as well as French. The following is just a sample   a fuller list is available from the WFA or from the Comité Regional du Tourisme de Picardie, 3 Rue Vincent Auriol, 80000 Amiens. Tel: 0033 322 91 10 15. There is also a tourist office in the basilica square in Albert.

HOTELS:

The Royal Picardie, Route d Amiens, 80300 Albert
Tel +33 322 75 37 00
Hotel de la Basilique, 3-5 Rue Gambetta, 80300 Albert
Tel +33 322 75 04 71
Relais Fleuri, 56 Avenue Faidherbe, 80300 Albert
Tel +33 322 75 08 11
Grande Hotel de la Paix, 43 Rue Victor Hugo, 80300 Albert
Tel +33 322 75 01 64

I have stayed in this latter hotel on many occasions over the years and have found it tremendously friendly with an excellent restaurant.

B & B Accommodation:

These can be seasonal and closed over some of the winter months (usually after the 11 November commemorations) so please check first before you set off if you are planning a winter tour.

Auchonvillers

Les Galets, Route de Beaumont, 80560 Auchonvillers
Tel/Fax +33 322 76 28 79

This house, run by Julie and Michael Renshaw, is just behind the old British front line before Beaumont Hamel. It is ideal for anyone wanting interesting walks along parts of the 1916 front – whether over Redan Ridge or to the Newfoundland Park. The rooms are all en suite, the breakfast is substantial, evening meals are available (except on Sunday) and there are comfortable sitting areas and lovely grounds.

Avril Williams, 10 Rue de Lattre,
Auchonvillers.
Tel +33 322 76 23 66

This is a large former farmhouse in the village, with a most interesting cellar and a proprietress who bubbles over with enthusiasm. The rooms are all en suite, and a substantial breakfast is served. Evening meals (also substantial) are available. There is now an attached tea room, and so it is possible to get lunch here as well.

Kieron Murphy and Paul Reed,
Sommecourt, 39 Grande Rue, 80300 Courcelette
Tel + 33 322 74 01 35

Nearer to Delville Wood, this is also housed in a former farm house. It boasts a resident battlefield expert and a contributing author to the series!

There are numerous others, amongst them a British one in Martinpuich, and French equivalents in Mailly Maillet, another at the crossroads where the Auchonvillers road meets the Serre road and in Grandcourt. It is also possible to hire cottages, details of which are often published in the various WFA publications. There is a camp site in Authuille, and another one below that village, near the banks of the Ancre.

I can strongly recommend the Auberge in Authuille, but it is best to book. Tel +33 322 75 15 18 (or if ringing locally, 0322...).

This concludes an awful lot of advice; it is not meant to deter but is the result of years of battlefield visiting and is designed to make your time trouble free and enjoyable.

Useful addresses:

The Imperial War Museum, Lambeth Road, London SE1 6H2
Tel: 0171 416 5000

The National Army Museum, Royal Hospital Road, Chelsea, London SW3 4HT
Tel: 0171 730 0717

The Commonwealth War Graves Commission, 2 Marlow Road, Maidenhead, Berks.
Tel: 01628 634221

The Western Front Association, PO Box 1914, Reading, Berks.
This address is for membership queries. Include a large (A4) s.a.e. envelope.

HOW TO USE THIS BOOK

For those of you who have never visited the battlefields I would recommend that you sit down with this book (and one or two others that I have recommended in the further reading section) in order to get a feel for the events and for the ground. This book covers the area over which a long drawn out battle was fought for a relatively small piece of ground; it offers a brief description of the fighting, followed by an in-depth description of just a few of the actions. It is by no means a comprehensive narrative of the events that took place in and around Delville Wood during the Great War. The best way to tour this battlefield is by foot, for that is how the soldier of the Great War saw it (albeit from trenches several feet deep), and it gives you a very good idea of the lie of the land. In turn this often helps to explain tactical decisions and events during the fighting. On the other hand, some of the distances involved can be great, so there is a car (or bike) tour included. Bear in mind that many of the roads had deeper embankments running alongside them; these have been reduced in height by road widening and metalling.

At the back of the book there is a section on car and walking tours. You would be advised to follow the car route round first so that you can get your bearings before engaging on the more detailed tours. There is a separate section for cemeteries and memorials.

This book is a guide to Longueval and Delville Wood; it does not set out to be a critical examination of this part of the Somme, nor even of this set of battles. Other books are readily available for what is probably the most written about battle in British military history, with all the controversies that follow on from this wealth of printed matter. What I would urge you to do, as you walk these fields, is to consider the problem not only from the view of those men in the trenches who did the fighting, but also the considerable difficulties facing the staffs and commanders. The secondary aim of this book is to be thought-provoking and to encourage the re-examination of whatever prejudices about the Great War that we might have. Considering the sacrifices that these men made, and the cost to the country in all manner of ways, it seems to me that an intelligent appraisal based on broad reading is the least we can do.

Chapter One

OUTLINE OF EVENTS:
14 JULY TO 31 AUGUST 1916

The story of the battle for Delville Wood in the summer of 1916 is a complex one. Below is a brief outline of what took place, the narrative assisted by the (generally) quite satisfactory maps from the Official History. The long days of July and August were filled with slogging matches between British, German and French forces in a complex battle pattern. The fight for Delville Wood was but one element in a colossal tussle, not only on the Somme but elsewhere on the Western Front – for example at Verdun and Fromelles. Also highly significant were the consequences of Brusilov's offensive on the

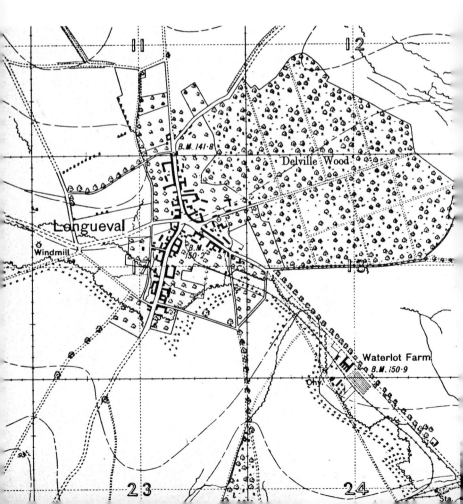

Eastern Front. Huge Russian advances caused considerable anxiety to the Germans, and indeed induced Roumania to enter the war on the Allied side. Finally Hindenburg stabilised the line, but at a cost of a total of two million casualties to both sides, the defeat of Roumania and the sacking of Falkenhayn, who fell a victim to his failures on both Fronts in 1916.

Attack at Dawn: 14 July 1916.

Delville Wood was the second objective for the attack of 9th Division, part of XIII Corps (commanded by Lieutenant-General Walter Congreve VC), itself to the right of XV Corps, in the famous dawn attack of 14 July 1916 against the Bazentin Ridge.

This attack is significant in a number of ways: the formulation of the plan; the moving of the troops into assembly positions and the preparation of those positions; the use of a short, preliminary artillery

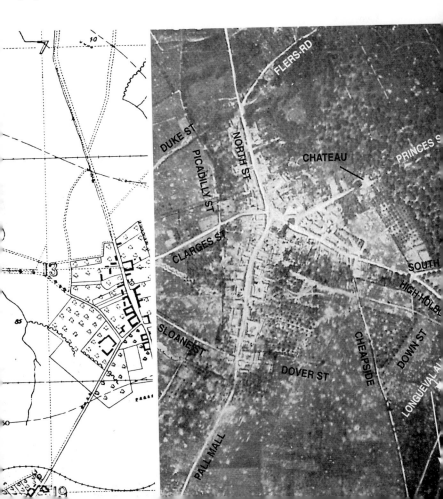

barrage of five minutes duration; the use of the creeping barrage without shrapnel but only using HE (high explosive) shells with delay fuzes; the attack at dawn; a significant action without the support of the French (though the French did fire a barrage across their own front at the outset of the battle); the fact that all bar one of the front line attacking battalions were New Army; the use of communications intercepts to deceive the enemy. All of these were either used for the first time or were a refinement of use on previous occasions and combine to make 14 July 1916 a most important date in the evolution of the British Expeditionary Force.

Given this large number of innovative fighting techniques, it is not altogether surprising that Rawlinson's original plan came in for some severe examination. Haig was not at all happy with it and tried to modify it considerably; however, as the preparations went ahead and reports of the progress made in preparing for the battle became clear, he gave his assent to widening the scope from an attack merely by one

George V on his visit to the Somme battlefields with a group of generals including Rawlinson and Congreve.

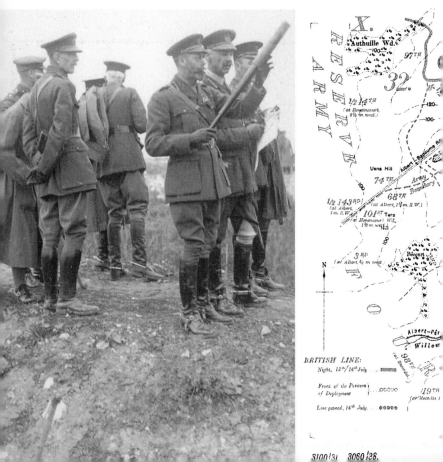

corps (XV) to include also a simultaneous attack by XIII Corps.

Against those who would use this instance as an example of Haig's unwillingness to try innovatory techniques, it is worth noting what the French thought of such a scheme. The French Sixth Army, under the command of General Fayolle, repeatedly urged that the attack be not attempted, an attack they regarded as sheer madness. Spears, the British liaison officer with General Balfourier, commanding the French XX Corps, on the British right, told Major-General Montgomery, Rawlinson's chief of staff, that the French regarded a night approach in preparation for a dawn attack as quite impossible for such inexperienced troops. Montgomery (not the same as his more famous namesake in World War II) replied to Spears,

> Tell General Balfourier, with my compliments, that if we are not on Longueval ridge at eight tomorrow morning I will eat my hat.

On being informed of the British success on the day by his liaison officer, Captain Sérot (*'Ils ont osé; ils ont reussi'*), Balfourier replied, *'Alors, le général Montgomery ne mange pas son chapeau'*.[1]

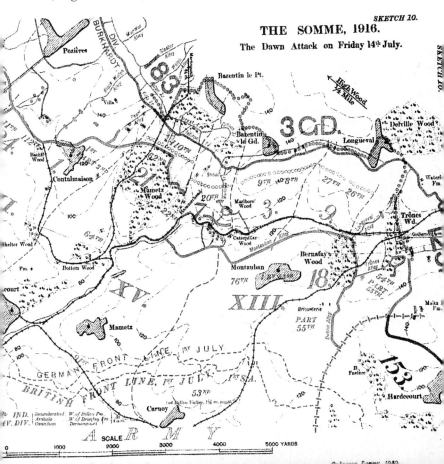

SKETCH 10.

THE SOMME, 1916.
The Dawn Attack on Friday 14th July.

In addition to factors listed above, success on the day also lay in large measure in the complete domination of the skies by the Royal Flying Corps. The Germans were unable to see what was going on as the British brought forward ammunition dumps into Caterpillar Valley, then guns and marked out approaches and line-up positions. German officer prisoners explained that their lack of patrolling in the lead up to the attack was due to the fact that there were no reliable NCOs left to lead them.[2]

This is not the place to discuss the successes and lost opportunities of 14 July; but I think that it is valid to have spent time briefly looking at the innovations to show that the British could learn rapidly from their mistakes and take military initiatives which were to be of long-term importance.

The 9th Division attacked with two brigades up (26 and 27), each with two battalions in the front and two in support. By about ten in the morning all of the immediate objectives were captured (which took them to the edge of Delville Wood), except for a strongpoint to the south east of Longueval and another one to the north of the village. In addition, Waterlot Farm, or at least the sugar refinery that was given the name of a nearby farm, remained firmly in German hands.

The problem that faced the 9th Division was that it was not a powerful enough force to carry out its task, especially given the problems that followed with the fall (finally) of Trônes Wood to the 18th Division (see Michael Stedman's *Guillemont* in this series). This left the 9th Division with an open right flank to defend on top of its other problems, and this situation on the right of the attack was a significant factor in the failure to develop the success of the attack to the west.

Although XIII Corps reported on two occasions that the whole of Longueval had fallen, in both cases it had to withdraw this report and revise it to the capture of only the southern half of the village. At the end of the day the British had created a salient in their line of some 6,000 yards, vulnerable to attack from Flers and the cover offered by Longueval and Delville Wood. In particular, progress to the right of the new British line was threatened by this situation.

9th Division now had to consider the problems left from the first day's sharp fighting. Waterlot Farm needed to be secured – or, at the very least, the Germans removed, and this was done by means of a dawn attack on 15 July, with heavy fighting continuing for much of the day; the position was finally occupied and consolidated on 17 July.

The Ordeal of the South African Brigade, 15 – 21 July.

The Division now had to complete its objectives for the original attack – that is all of Longueval and Delville Wood. The Official History describes it as follows:

> The wood consisted of a thick tangle of trees, chiefly oak and birch, with dense hazel thickets intersected by grassy rides; covering about 156 acres, it filled the angle formed by the Flers and Ginchy roads, and, as its northern part lay on a reverse slope, the Germans had the advantage of a covered approach from the north-east into the far end of Longueval, which lay in a shallow depression.[3]

The author of 17/Royal Fusiliers history described it as,

> In shape Delville Wood resembled a dog's head, with the nose and muzzle pointing due east, thus forming a salient; the whole Wood formed a dangerous salient in the British line, which ran almost due south from the south-eastern corner to Maltz Horn Farm, and almost due west from the north and north-western outskirts to Pozieres.[4]

Early on 15 July 27 Brigade, reinforced by the 1st South African Regiment, attempted to capture Longueval, but were forced back. The rest of the South African Brigade was ordered to capture Delville Wood 'at all costs'; the attack consisted of little more than half the brigade, spearheaded by 2nd South African Regiment. The advance

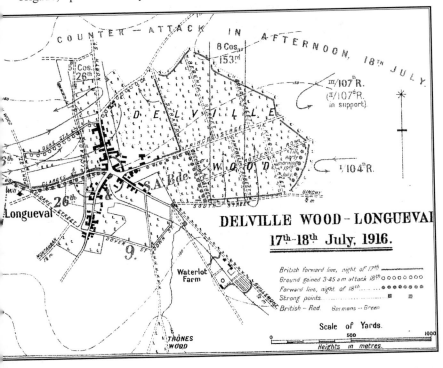

DELVILLE WOOD – LONGUEVAL
17th–18th July, 1916.

British forward line, night of 17th ⎯⎯⎯⎯
Ground gained 3·45 a.m attack 18th ०००००००
Forward line, night of 18th ●●●●●●●
Strong points ▣   ▣
British – Red.   Germans – Green

Scale of Yards.
0   500   1000

Heights in metres.

began at 6.15 am and after several hours the whole wood was captured, with the exception of very strong German positions in the north western corner of the wood – ie that point closest to the northern part of Longueval. An attempt was made to expel the Germans on the 16th, but this failed, and the attacking troops had also to endure unrelenting German shelling and localised counter-attacks. Further attempts on the 17th also failed, so that Congreve determined that the 9th Division should be replaced by the much fresher 3rd Division, who would make another attempt on the 18th, with a pre-dawn attack from the west.

The Germans, meanwhile, in line with Falkenhayn's edict that no ground should be surrendered, were making their own plans to recover the wood and the village.

During all this time Delville Wood had been saturated with a German bombardment of extraordinary ferocity and length. Members of 76 Brigade launched their attack at 3.45 am on 18 July from positions near the windmill, on the western edge of the village, and although they made contact with the South Africans in the wood, the whole position they gained had to be abandoned in the face of the German artillery onslaught. The by now exhausted and severely depleted South African, shattered and blasted, thirsty and tired – and now wet through because of heavy rain – faced a massive series of German attacks launched in the mid-afternoon of the 18th; this resulted in the recapture of much of Longueval, whilst the scattered remnant of South Africans hung on to a tiny part of the wood on the south eastern edge. A further British attack at 7.15 am on 19 July managed to restore control of the southern portion of the wood, but the situation in this sector remained distinctly unsatisfactory, and posed a significant obstacle to developments further south. Delville and High woods remained a problem for British arms for several crucial weeks in the summer of 1916.

If the British were having problems, so were the Germans. German accounts commented on the ferocity of the British barrage on 19 July, two regiments had been used up in the attacks (ie six battalions); the 26th regiment asked to be relieved, noting that,

See map
page 107

> *All the troops were exhausted, there were no leaders left, and*
> *fresh forces were necessary if the ground gained was to be held.*

In the early hours of 20 July, the 3rd Division replaced the 9th; the ordeal of the South Africans was almost over, but at the most tremendous cost. An attack by 76 Brigade, launched at 3.35 am, was confused and broke down, but at last they were able to relieve the last of the South Africans in the line. Their Brigade had gone in with 121 officers and 3,032 other ranks; only 29 officers and 751 other ranks answered the roll when it was called on 21st July. The 9th Division suffered 314 officer and 7,203 other rank casualties in the first three weeks of July. The German 26th Regiment was reduced from approximately 2,700 all ranks to 10 officers and 250 other ranks; the wood had been a killing ground for both sides.

The problem of the capture of Delville Wood was similar to that faced in the horrendous struggle to take Trônes Wood. Pre-war doctrine dictated that woods should be enveloped by taking the ground on either side of them, but for various reasons this was not practicable in these cases (and, indeed, elsewhere on the Somme). The result was that vast artillery resources by both sides could be concentrated on the woods, with devastating consequences for the infantry, often victims to their own artillery and machine-gun barrage support.

The Long Slog: 23 July – 3 September

After a pause for reorganisation, the assault recommenced on 23 July; XIII Corps had two divisions in the attack, the 30th Division concerned with Guillemont, the 3rd with Delville Wood and Longueval. Again, the attack came from the west; again there were problems with orders reaching a number of units in adequate time; again early successes were reversed by vigorous German counter-attacks. The British found themselves back in their original positions

See map
page 109

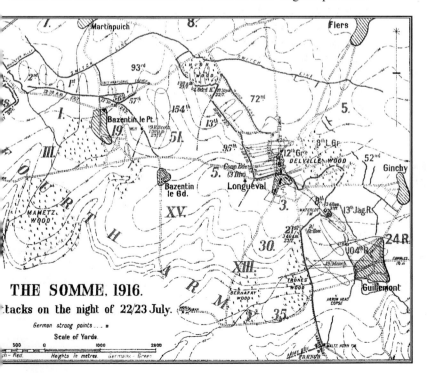

THE SOMME, 1916.

tacks on the night of 22/23 July.

Germans strong points .... ▪
Scale of Yards.
500   0   1000   2000
h – Red.   Heights in metres.   Germans Green

at the end of the day; whilst their brigade commander (Brigadier-General Potter of 95 Brigade) was wounded whilst coming forward to try and find out just what was happening in the attack area.

It is important, in understanding the development of the Battle of the Somme, not to be completely focussed at any one stage on a particular part of the battlefront – for there were three large formations involved: besides Rawlinson's Fourth Army, there was Gough's Fifth Army and the French Sixth Army. Chris McCarthy's *The Somme, The Day-by-Day Account* helps, by its daily summary, to keep a bigger picture in mind.

On 24 July Haig arrived at Rawlinson's Headquarters at Querrieu and held talks with Rawlinson and Foch at which he emphasised the vital importance of securing Longueval and Delville Wood, not merely as being important to the British, but securing them from the Germans. These positions were essential for the German defence of the southern part of the battlefield, providing vital springboards for counter-attacking thrusts. The next attack would be a joint operation by XIII and XV Corps, which were tasked to clear the area in one operation.

See map page 110

3rd Division was replaced by the 2nd (recently serving with First Army) on the night of 25 July; 5th Division from XV Corps remained on the left. The attack was to be launched at 7.10 am on 27 July, preceded by a massive, hour-long, artillery bombardment. This had a

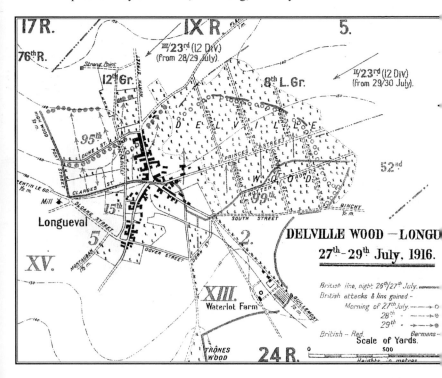

DELVILLE WOOD — LONGU
27th – 29th July, 1916.

British line, night 26th/27th July.
British attacks & line gained –
Morning of 27th July.
28th
29th
British – Red.   Germans –
Scale of Yards.
0   500

very considerable effect on the defenders – understandably. As soon as the bombardment opened up, some sixty Germans rushed forward to surrender to men of 99 Brigade. Advancing troops found a scene of indescribable horror when they advanced through to Princes Street, some ten minutes after the attack began. Numerous machine-guns lay smashed, surrounded by numerous dead and wounded defenders – presumably intermingled with the corpses of the South Africans who had held the trench during their ordeal of a week earlier. The attack went forward relatively smoothly, though one wants to beware looking at such actions with the dispassion of passing years and the ignorance of the horror of fighting. There were numerous casualties from well-placed German machine-guns, but substantial progress was made at relatively small cost. To the right, 15 Brigade of 5th Division also made good progress, albeit after substantial casualties had been caused in the forming-up trenches by a pre-assault German bombardment. The Germans remained in possession of the northern part of Longueval, but they were now in a very difficult position, as the British line had advanced on either side of them. Over the next two days the line gradually inched its way further eastwards, as the Germans gave up ground at painful cost to both sides. The 5th (German) Division had suffered, for example, some five thousand casualties in the two weeks or so that it held the line in and near Delville Wood before it was relieved on 3 August.

A large attack on 30 July on the Fourth Army front was directed to the east of Delville Wood – aimed at High Wood. The situation was still very confused in Longueval, and only small gains were made in a subsidiary attack to the north east of the village. Most of Fourth Army's efforts over the next days were concentrated on Guillemont. 2nd Division, now manning the whole of the Longueval and Delville Wood front, was relieved gradually over the first days of August by the 17th (Northern) Division, a task made extremely difficult by the chaos in Delville Wood, where the line was not at all clear and where the German positions were very close.

It engaged in a number of attacks to improve the line across the whole of the Longueval sector. An attack launched in the early hours of 4 August was a costly failure; whilst another on the 7th, to push the line of British outposts beyond the wood, also failed. However some advances were made in front of Longueval itself. What these attacks showed was that the Germans had made improvements in their own trench positions.

On the night of 12 August the 17th Division (having suffered just

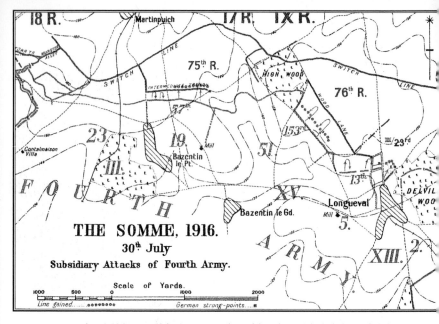

THE SOMME, 1916.
30th July
Subsidiary Attacks of Fourth Army.

Scale of Yards.

Line gained...... ●●●●●●●   German strong-points.... ■

under 1600 casualties) was replaced by the 14th (Light) Division.

The *Official History* gives a bleak summary of August 1916.

> *There was little to encourage or inspire the troops of all arms who fought on the Somme in August: subjected to heavy loss, great hardships, and tremendous physical and moral strain, they had only their own dogged spirit to maintain them.*[5]

The battle of 14 July had considerably improved the capacity of the British and French to operate effectively together on the right of the attack, but it was vital that the line Ginchy-Guillemont-Falfemont Farm be secured before a further general move forward would be practicable. Haig therefore urged that careful preparations be made on the right of Fourth Army before a further big attack was made. This was to be on 7 August, later amended to the 8th. This fighting, largely completely unsuccessful, did not involve any considerable new British action in Delville Wood. The most significant problem facing the British, the Official History notes,

> *was how best to deal with the German machine-guns hidden in shell-holes and portions of shattered trench and amongst the débris and rubble of what had been Guillemont. They were as difficult to locate as they were to destroy; and, although the German system of defence laboured under grave disadvantages as regards control and supply, it was only too effective so long as the machine-gunners possessed the spirit and tenacity to hold on under the strain of continuous bombardment.*[6]

30

A casualty of the persistent, slogging fighting since 14 July was Congreve, who gave up his command due to ill health; he was replaced by Lieutenant-General the Earl of Cavan of XIV Corps on 10 August. In due course the staff of XIII Corps was replaced by that of Cavan, and on 17 August XIII Corps was restyled XIV.

Joffre had been unhappy for some time with the strategically insignificant but bloody battles to which the Somme had been reduced; and he proposed a further joint attack on 22 August; this would be preceded by another British attack against positions on the right of Fourth Army on the 18th.

The 14th Division (in XV Corps) undertook the Delville Wood part of the attack; 43 Brigade was to take the line from the northern part of ZZ Trench to the German position in Princes Street. There was very considerable fighting, including the inevitable German counter-attacks and most of the objectives (especially on the right) were taken and consolidated. The rest of the wood was not attacked, except by a screen of artillery, whilst 41 Brigade

Lieut-Gen the Earl of Cavan

took the line beyond Orchard trench. The German position in the wood remained, but was gradually being enveloped by British advances on either side.

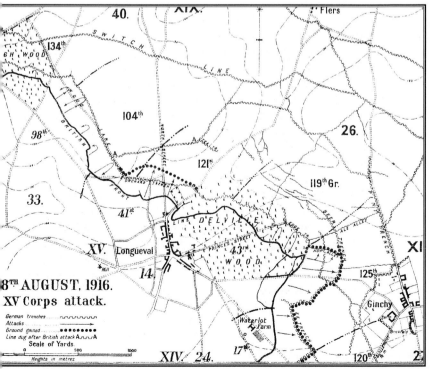

The Wood finally captured: 19 August – 3 September

On 17 August GHQ informed Rawlinson that the 'Tank' would be available for a new offensive in mid-September; therefore some three weeks remained to get to the proposed start line. Amongst other requirements, XV Corps would be required to clear the northern edge of Delville Wood. On 21 August an attempt by 8/KRRC to occupy posts in the German front line in the wood was foiled at the cost of heavy casualties (200 men) and no gain. A more considerable effort was made on 24 August. Again 8/KRRC (41 Brigade), on the right of the divisional attack, had difficulty making progress, and were stopped before Ale Alley. Almost everywhere else the attack by men of 42 Brigade was successful, and the Germans were more or less ejected from the wood; on 25 August 9/Rifle Brigade cleared Edge Trench almost as far as Ale Alley. It fell to 10/DLI to launch a surprise attack on the afternoon of 27 August which finally removed the Germans from Delville Wood for the first time; their tenuous grip in posts in Edge Trench was finally broken.

On the morning of 31 August 14 Division was relieved in the wood by the 24th. August had cost the 14th Division some 3,600 casualties; its Royal Engineer Field Company (89) had lost fifty percent of its men and nearly all its officers in the ten days it spent working in Delville Wood, clearing and consolidating positions there.

The men of 24th Division were not to enjoy a peaceful time. The Germans launched a series of attacks, commencing at 1 pm on 31 August and ending some seven or eight hours later. Each attack was

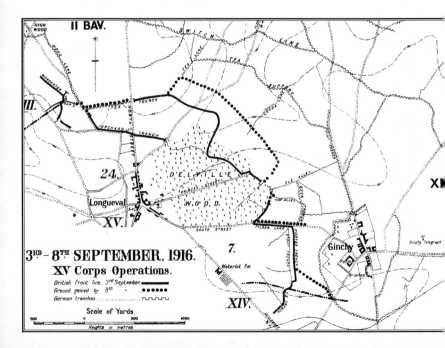

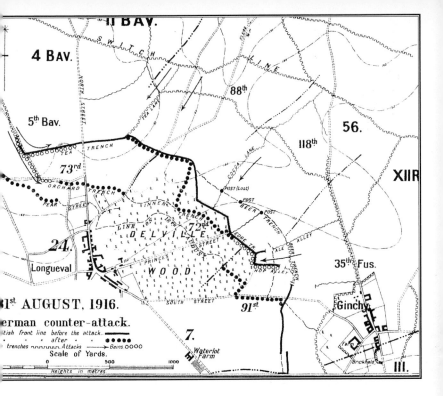

interspersed by ferocious shelling of the British line. Some ground was given on the right, and the situation was quite serious for a while on the Division's left, but towards evening the German efforts had petered out; their attack did leave them, once more, with a foothold in what was still called a wood, although all trees had long since been blasted to oblivion. It was not until the attacks of 3 September, part of what is known as the Battle of Guillemont, that Delville Wood was finally secured. An account of the events of these days around Ginchy is provided by Michael Stedman's forthcoming *Ginchy* in this series.[7]

1. Brigadier-General Sir James E Edmonds, Official History *Military Operations France and Belgium.* (Hereafter OH 1916) Vol II, pp. 82-83
2. *OH 1916,* Vol II pp. 68-69
3. *OH 1916,* Vol II p. 91
4. Everard Wyrall, *The 17th (S.) Battalion Royal Fusiliers 1914-1919.* Methuen and Co Ltd., 1930.
5. *OH 1916,* Vol II p.174
6. *OH 1916,* Vol II pp. 180-181
7. This chapter is based on the narrative found in the appropriate parts of *OH 1916*. The reader is warned that the General Index references in the Official History are far from being comprehensive. Thus Delville Wood is given only one page reference in Volume II!

Chapter Two

14 – 18 JULY 1916:
THE ATTACK OF THE 9th (Scottish) DIVISION

Preliminaries: Artillery and the Start Line

The 9th Division's CRA (Commander, Royal Artillery) was Brigadier-General HH Tudor. He was responsible for an imaginative artillery plan encompassing the best practices that had emerged from British and French experience; he went on, in the latter days of the war (from March 1918), to command this Division.

He appreciated that the biggest problem that he faced was Delville Wood. Shrapnel shells, by hitting the trees, burst prematurely and therefore were as big a threat to the attacking infantry as for the

Brigadier-General HH Tudor

defenders. The artillery bombardment was due to be fired at zero plus five; he therefore decided to use shrapnel but, after three minutes, to use HE shells only. The point about this was that high explosive shells had delay action, so that the shell would not go off until it was set so to do, regardless of any obstructions it might find in its path. Secondly, the lessons of the first day of the Somme had been learnt, and instead of a barrage that lifted well beyond the enemy front line at zero, a creeping barrage, in a series of fifty yard lifts every one and a half minutes, was to be used. This aimed to keep the Germans in the shelter of their trenches and away from manning their machine-guns until the advancing infantry, under the wall of fire, was almost upon them. To give some idea of the complexity of the artillery programme, Tudor had set down a programme of eight separate barrages.

1st Barrage: 5 minutes till Zero.
2nd Barrage: Zero minus five
3rd Barrage: Zero minus five until minus forty-five
4th Barrage: Zero minus forty-five until minus ninety
5th Barrage: Zero minus ninety until minus one hundred and twenty
The remaining barrages were meant to cover the attack on Delville Wood:
6th Barrage: Zero minus one hundred and twenty until one hundred and fifty
7th Barrage: Zero minus one hundred and fifty until two hundred and thirty four
8th Barrage: from then on.

The other problem that Tudor faced was that the 9th Division was the right hand formation of the 14 July attack, and so he had to provide adequate artillery cover to what promised to be a troublesome right flank. The German defences in and around Waterlot Farm were to be

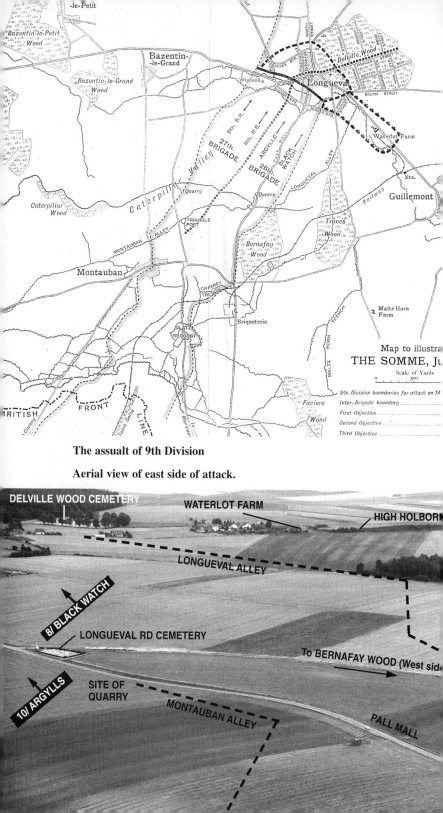

The assualt of 9th Division

Aerial view of east side of attack.

kept under artillery fire, as this portion of the line to be attacked was not to be tackled until later. This was mainly due to the fact that at the time of the attack Trones Wood was still in German hands and would provide devastating defensive fire.

The Division, as for the others in the attack, also had to get all the assaulting troops out into position in the dark. In order to do this, marker tapes had to be laid during the limited hours of the night. 26 (Highland) Brigade was to attack on the right. It was brought to the northern slopes of Caterpillar Valley, its left boundary being the track from Montauban to Longueval. The marker party consisted of the Brigade Major and the adjutants of 8/Black Watch and 10/Argylls, along with forty markers. The markers were to work from the left flank of each battalion; thus the left markers of the Black Watch worked their way up the Bernafay Wood to Longueval road (labelled on Trench Maps Pall Mall) and the Argylls up the Montauban to Longueval track. The Black Watch left a pair of men at intervals of seventy yards, so that at the end the final markers were about five hundred yards short of the German line. Once in position, one of the pair would set off at right angles with a tape 150 yards long, which fixed the right of the wave or platoon. The Argylls carried out a similar procedure on their track; at 12.25 am the relevant battalions moved up in single file, and as they reached the appropriate marker, platoons fixed bayonets and moved to the right. The Brigade was in position by 3 am without any problem.

27 (Lowland) Brigade went though a similar process. At about 11 pm Major Teacher, the Brigade Major, and three others laid a central tape between the two roads that marked the flanks of the Brigade: on the right the Montauban to Longueval track, on the left the road from the Quarry to the Windmill to the west of Longueval. At 1.45 am 11/Royal Scots, 9/Scottish Rifles and 12/Royal Scots moved off to their assault positions, all of which was achieved with only five casualties. The most serious loss was Lieutenant Colonel HL Budge of 12/Royal Scots, who was mortally wounded by a shell fragment on the west side of Montauban. He died of his wounds soon afterwards, and is buried in Carnoy Military Cemetery.

Lieut-Colonel H L Budge, 12 Battalion, The Royal Scots.

37

The Attack

In general the results of the attack went according to plan. 8/Black Watch faced considerable problems from a German machine-gun nest positioned on the south east corner of Longueval; this in turn was covered by two German field guns on the south western edge of Delville Wood, on the Longueval side of the present car park for the South African Memorial. This machine-gun post was not finally subdued until 5 pm. However, some men from the Battalion managed to penetrate further into Delville Wood than had been envisaged, taking up positions in Buchanan Street. These had to be abandoned however, as they were without any support on the left flank. By midday the Battalion held a line from the square north of the church south east to within a hundred yards distance of the west of South Street, the road which now runs past the Memorial car park and Delville Wood Military Cemetery. In the course of the afternoon patrols, which had been pushed forward into the wood, came across stiffening German resistance.

The Argylls were completely successful. The leading companies passed over the German Front Line whilst those behind cleared it. Some men got ahead of the British barrage, and had to take shelter in shell-holes, entertained (if that is the word) by a piper playing the regimental march. The Battalion took Clarges Street with minimal resistance, cleared the houses on the west side of the main street (Pall Mall) and consolidated their position. C Company assisted 11/Royal Scots, who had been held up by uncut German wire. They bombed along the German line northwards, and drove the defenders across the front of the advancing 27 Brigade.

The right battalion of 27 Brigade, 11/Royal Scots, had difficulty with the wire, as mentioned above, and there were casualties as attempts were made to cut it under accurate German machine-gun fire. Assisted by accurate Lewis gun fire, the actions of their neighbouring battalion and the action of A Company, which found a way through the wire and bombed down the German line, the Battalion took its objectives and managed to bag 63 German prisoners.

To their left 9/Scottish Rifles had a relatively easy passage, and indeed were able to offer assistance to the left battalion of the 3rd Division, which had themselves been held up by problems with uncut German wire.

This Brigade had a fairly complex manoeuvre to carry out; 9/Scottish Rifles were to hold a position to the south of the Bazentin to Longueval road whilst 11/Royal Scots became the effective left hand battalion by continuing the advance and occupying Duke Street between Pont Street and Piccadilly, which they did. 12/Royal Scots was to come through the 11th's first objective and wheel east to complete the capture of the village, holding the line from the corner of Duke Street and Piccadilly to the point on Princes Street where it emerged from the western end of the wood. The Battalion had lost its commanding officer, and there was confusion. The Germans were sniping accurately from Piccadilly and the orchards to its immediate east, as well as bringing machine-gun fire to bear. Eventually 12/Royal Scots dug a line facing east, with its right flank in touch with the Argylls on Clarges Street and its left in contact with 11/Royal Scots position. 27 Brigade had not reached its second objective.

The divisional commander, Major-General Furse, had been able to exert control over his men – indeed it was he that had ordered neighbouring battalions to assist those held up by the uncut wire – but communications became increasingly difficult as the battle progressed. The part of 12/Royal Scots in the battle plan was crucial:

> *The possession of the Longueval plateau was the key to the operations against High Wood in the north, and if the village was not taken, the plans of Sir Douglas Haig would be thrown out of gear. Moreover it was from Longueval that the attack on Delville Wood was to be launched; without it the operation would be more intricate.*[1]

Furse therefore decided to place the 1st South African Infantry under the command of 27 Brigade; he warned Brigadier-General Lukin that his South African Brigade would have to take Delville Wood as 26 Brigade would need all its resources to capture Waterlot Farm.

The failure of 12/Royal Scots had to be rectified. But Longueval, as many of the German held villages of the battlefield, provided real problems for the attackers.

> *It was clear that the northern part of Longueval could not be cleared by a casual or haphazard attack. The enclosed nature of the oblong of orchards made it difficult to locate the enemy's posts with certainty, and the artillery were handicapped by the want of a post from which to observe the fire. The problem was in fact more intricate than was realised at the time. The battering that the village had received from our guns had only been sufficient to convert it into a stronghold of immense strength. Amidst the jagged and tumbled masonry the defenders had numerous well-protected corners from which they could fire without being detected, and the oblong was full of shelters where*

Germans near the main square of Longueval in the halcyon days before the Somme offensive commenced.

> *the garrison could take refuge from the fire of field guns. The whole area needed to be pulverised by heavy shells, as General Furse realised. Against infantry alone the place was virtually impregnable, since the scope for manoeuvring was limited and all the approaches were swept by the fire of the defenders.*[2]

The Story of 11th and 12th Royal Scots.[3]

Brigadier-General William Denman Croft was a quite extraordinary soldier. In the course of the Great War he earned four DSOs and was mentioned in despatches ten times; before the war he had been severely wounded in 1907 by a poisoned arrow whilst serving in Nigeria. In the early months of the war he served as adjutant with 5/Scottish Rifles before being given command of 11/Royal Scots in December 1915; in the middle of September 1917 he was given command of 27 (Lowland) Brigade, with whom he remained until the end of the war. He remained a professional soldier, transferring in due course to the Tank Corps, established the Cornwall district of the Home Guard in World War II and died in his ninetieth year in 1968. He wrote a well known account of his time with the 9th Division of a type that is probably unfashionable amongst certain circles now, but probably reflects many of the attitudes held by a majority of the officers of his time. Certainly it portrays a man who cared deeply for his men in both his battalion and brigade. His description of the events of 14 July and leading up to them is no exception.

> *We went back to Billon Wood to wash and brush up for the coming battle. Here I was ordered to go sick by our brigade commander.*

However it wasn't likely that one would go back with our big battle in prospect, and so I managed to stay out of the way until we started for our night march. And the dear old chap was too busy to notice me. Never would I have forgiven myself for missing that battle. For on the 14th July 1916, the British Army performed one of the finest feats which have ever been done in

Enjoying a smoke and a bite close to the front line.

war; to wit, a night march to a position of deployment within 500 yards of a vigilant enemy, then a crawl forward on hands and knees, to be followed at zero by the assault of a strongly wired and entrenched position which had suffered no previous bombardment to shake the moral of the defenders. And, in addition, Trones Wood on our right rear, in fact very nearly directly behind us, was as yet uncaptured!

The cool daring of the thing ensured its success. And how it appealed to our lads! This was the sort of business for which they had joined up, not brutal, bloody murder, to which they had been accustomed for over a year. [The 9th Division had had a hard time, not least at Loos, where they had the dubious distinction of not only having their divisional commander, Major-General Thesiger, killed in action, but they failed to recover his body afterwards.] *'Always endeavour to surprise and mystify your enemy,' should be, and must be, the soldier's first maxim, otherwise he s not likely to be much of a success in a war. I shall never as long as I live forget starting out on that great venture. On nearing Montauban, where the Boche was indulging in his usual antics, the whole brigade got into single file. We were*

leading battalion, and were fortunate enough to miss the shelling of the western outskirts of the village. But alas, it came down on 12/Royal Scots who were immediately behind us, and got their colonel – Budge...Had he lived, his fine battalion under his able leadership would have undoubtedly succeeded in [their difficult] *task; but it was not to be, and Longueval was not finally cleared of the enemy for some weeks. Even now one cannot speak without deep regret and sorrow for one of the finest regimental officers in the army. He knew he was to die, knew it perfectly well; his one hope was that he would die in the hour of victory.*

On reaching Caterpillar Valley, a thousand yards in advance of our front line, we met Norman Teacher, our brigade major, cool and alert as ever. He

42

had been engaged throughout the night in watching the Boche trenches with a party of scouts; a ticklish job, and he was mightily relieved to see us. There wasn't much time to waste, and we were barely in position before the move forward began. As one had a last look round, and passed a word or two with old friends, one little thought how few would be standing up in a short time. I spoke to Lemmy about his communications – he was now signalling officer – and I never saw him alive again. [Lieutenant PG Lemmey is buried in Quarry Cemetery, II.A.6. There are a number of other 11/Royal Scots there as well – originally they were buried at Quarry Scottish cemetery.]

We found our wire uncut, all in the dark, remember, when men's nerves are prone to falter. But the officers and NCOs went gallantly forward to the business of wire-cutting in the face of a cruel machine-gun , promptly taken on by Winkle – gallant old Winkle [His name was actually Lieutenant Winchester] with his two Lewis guns. In less time than it takes to write about it he had them cold, firing high over our heads at first, and later silent.

An artist's impression of the assault on Longueval.

The Argylls were on our right, and I shall never forget their old pipe-major strutting up and down a certain well-sniped road near the village, while we cowered in a ditch alongside. Someone pulled him down eventually, and his colonel sent him back to the transport lines, from which he made several attempts to get back to his battalion.

Our leading companies were right on their mark; but the wheel of 12/Royal Scots did not come off, as Budge and most of their officers were knocked out. The men went forward, a gallant mob with no leaders, into the village. But they did not know what to do when they got there.

We found the Scottish Rifles had secured our left flank. And so, under galling fire from snipers in apple trees, we dug ourselves in with speed. We had sustained heavy losses, for Henry and Jack Cowan had been killed at the wire; [Captain JT Henry MC, commemorated on the Thiepval Memorial; Captain JOC Cowan, buried in Quarry Cemetery, II.C.1] *(two other company commanders) were wounded and missing respectively. Then Mabin, temporarily commanding the Bart.'s company, was killed later on in the morning, in the place where he knew he was fated to die.* [Captain JJ Maybin is buried in Quarry Cemetery, III.A.6. Earlier on in his book, Croft had commented on this premonition (pp. 13 – 14): 'He was absolutely positive that he would be killed at a certain place, which he accurately described to a friend. The friend, on hearing of his death, sent me Mabin's [sic] description, which I was able to verify.] *And their Highlanders had suffered even more than we had. What their casualties were I never knew: but Scotland knew.*

11/Royal Scots suffered over 600 casualties and 24 officers – most of those in the first hour of the attack. Croft goes on in his book to highlight a fact about Longueval that is strangely absent from many of the official accounts.

There were some subterranean passages right through the village of Longueval against which it was rather difficult to compete. The Boche had entrances well on his side of the village, and when things got a bit too warm for him down he would pop like a sewer rat by means of bolt holes in most of the houses. He nearly got the combined battalion headquarters of the Seaforths and Watch. It was at night, and they were having food, when one of the battalion runners who had been nosing about suddenly rushed in to say that the Boches were next door. As their front

line was some considerable way in advance this was particularly
cheering intelligence.

Longueval and Delville Wood were (and presumably still are) honeycombed with a number of passages. It is rumoured that some of the system is big enough to allow the proverbial coach and horses drive through it. It seems reasonably certain that the Germans evacuated much of the civilian population via the Presbytery and the Church out to the Flers road (emerging in the sunken part north of Delville Wood) through a tunnel, running under the chateau grounds and the wood; whilst others were removed from Waterlot Farm via a similar system that connected to this one under the wood. Such systems would have been enormously useful to the Germans in their defence of the sector.

12/Royal Scots, as is evident from above, had had a torrid time of things. The regimental history notes,

> *The men felt as if they had been fighting for hours, yet it was*
> *not 7 am; in this short time the battalion had lost nearly 50 per*
> *cent of its strength, and only seven officers, all of them second*
> *lieutenants, were in the front line.*

In the circumstances, it is extraordinary how strongly the 12/Royal Scots persevered with their task – indeed it is a facet of the Great War how men on all sides were prepared to throw themselves into almost certain death in order to carry out their perceived duty. At 7 am two companies, A and D, charged once more and got within fifty yards of Piccadilly before they halted before the irresistible hurdle of machine-gun fire.

> *It was sun-clear that a frontal assault against Piccadilly was*
> *suicidal, so the 12th next tried to carry the rectangle by an*
> *advance from Clarges Street. Second Lieutenants Armit and*
> *Noble, having mustered three sections with one Lewis gun,*
> *attacked Piccadilly and North Street from the south. The*
> *principal attempt was directed against North Street, at the*
> *junction of which with Clarges Street we had erected a barrier.*
> *Passing through this the Royal Scots came under a withering fire*
> *as soon as they entered the hostile area. Every ruin housed at*
> *least one machine-gun, and to escape the sputtering lead the*
> *men had to cower under the broken masonry that lined both*
> *sides of the street. The Boches had every advantage; they*
> *occupied positions that could not be precisely located, and they*
> *commanded all the cleared spaces that the assailants had to*
> *traverse if they intended to push home their attack. The 12th had*
> *no option but to retire, and it was not without incurring many*

perils that they reached the friendly side of the barricade.

The 1st South African Infantry was brought up to attempt to clear the village. It managed to get to the new front held by the two other brigades of the Division without a single casualty, despite approaching over ground that was swept by German artillery. Spread out, it advanced through the village, reaching its first objectives just before 4 pm, but once more German sniper and machine-gun fire halted the attack. Patrols were sent out and discovered that the whole of the northern part of the village was held by a great number of machine-guns. The regiment stayed in position at the front, but resumed its place in the South African Brigade on the morning of the 15th.

The South Africans had as their task the clearance of Delville Wood. Their heroic struggle will be covered in a subsequent chapter.

27 (Lowland) Brigade: 15 – 18 July 1916.

See map
page 14

The significance of the Longueval plateau is shown by the map on page 14 – the ground on which it lay was the key for much of the Anglo-French advance (and conversely the German defence) on the southern part of the battlefield of the Somme.

The regimental history of the Royal Scots takes up the story.

Throughout the night of the 14/15 July the noise and screams of bursting shells formed a sinister counterpoint to the activities of the troops in the battle area. In the trench systems men were at work with pick and shovel, while in the hinterland hordes of parties carrying stores and rations braved numerous gusts of shell fire as they carried out their missions. It is to the credit of the Quartermasters and the Transport Officers and their staffs that they never allowed any difficulties to prevent them from delivering the food and other stores that they knew were urgently needed by the men in the trenches. Under the prevailing conditions sleep was practically impossible for anyone near the front, and when the 15th July dawned the crinkled faces of the troops showed how heavy was the strain to which they were being subjected.

Once more 12/Royal Scots were called upon to carry Longueval. Another bombardment was fired before, at 11 am, three sections attacked. One came from the west, and was soon stopped by the defenders' fire. The other two bombed their way from house to house along North Street, and at one stage seemed to have carried the rectangle. The attackers dropped off a small garrison as each building was taken and reached a point halfway to Duke Street when they were halted at a clearing in between the houses; the Germans had cleared the area so that it could be swept by fire.

Even those parts that had been captured had to be abandoned, as the German artillery removed the defenders by the sheer persistence and vehemence of their fire. In the evening of the 15th they had to fall back to the barricade.

At 7.30 pm two of the remaining five officers, Second Lieutenants Noble and Armit, led two groups, respectively into the orchards from Clarges Street and the other up North Street.

The former group, moving with some difficulty through the tangled undergrowth, had progressed about 100 yards when it reached a thick hedge beyond which it was impossible to advance. The first men who tried to wriggle through it at once became the target of rifle and machine-gun fire. The North Street thrust was also a failure, but Second Lieutenant Armit and his party had the satisfaction of dropping a number of the enemy by the fire of a Lewis gun. The battalion had now reached the limit of exhaustion, but though the men were too weary to assault they were still able to deal shrewdly with any attack that was directed against them. About 11 pm some Germans emerged from the direction of the rectangle with the intention of making a counter-attack, expecting probably that the Royal Scots would be so discouraged by their repeated rebuffs that they would not offer any effective resistance. They were rudely disillusioned; the

The key to much of the fighting in Delville Wood lay in the outstanding performance of the machine-gun teams of both sides.

> *Royal Scots opened such a galling fire that the attack swiftly melted away.*

11/Royal Scots had had a relatively uneventful 15 July, albeit under persistent harassing fire as they attempted to consolidate and develop their position. Once more the 1st South African Infantry was attached to the Brigade for this attack. At 10 am the 11/Royal Scots and the 1st South African Infantry (on the right) were to launch an attack from the line Princes – Clarges streets, using two companies from each battalion, whilst B Company of the Royal Scots created a diversion to the west. Croft writes,

> *It was very difficult to reconnoitre owing to the sniping; however we gave them a really good doing with Stokes and that funny old trench mortar which looked like half a dumb bell, and then we attacked with one company, while another was ready to exploit as soon as the leading company gave them room to manoeuvre. South Africans were attacking on our right, more in Delville Wood; as a matter of fact we had to finish up at the bottom of the hill. And as we were already commanding that side of the village it was not a particularly necessary operation from our point of view.*

> *We tried and tried all that day to cut through the impenetrable undergrowth stuffed with machine-guns, but our progress was slow and slight. The South Africans had no better fortune in the tangle, and late in the afternoon we gave up the attempt. Turner and Sergeant Allwright, afterwards adjutant of the 11/Royal Scots, had worked like Trojans, and I was satisfied that they had done all that was possible in the way of leadership. The men were splendid too, always responding gamely to the call of their leaders.*

It was the same clearing that had held up 12/Royal Scots that was to be the undoing of the attack by 11/Royal Scots. In addition, the nature of the ground made coherent movement extremely difficult. Ewing writes,

> *It was seamed with rows of thick and prickly hedges, and there was a profusion of tough undergrowth that wound round a man's legs like tentacles. The Germans had strengthened these natural obstructions by erecting belts of barbed wire concealed by the foliage and hedges. These barriers rendered a direct advance through the orchards well-nigh impossible.*

With the attack broken down, the men returned to the relative safety of their jumping-off positions. It was observed, however, that a number of wounded lay out in the ground near the German positions, in peril not only from their wounds, bullets and artillery but also from the relentless heat of the sun. Turner and Allwright went back to bring them in.

> [They] *crept cautiously into the orchards and hoisting the wounded men on their backs crawled with them into safety. Gusts of bullets stirred the undergrowth as they performed this noble feat, but by rare good fortune neither the officer nor the sergeant were hit.*

Croft commented on their feat,

> *Remember, these two had been on the rack for three days and three nights, and on top of that they had been fighting all day under close machine-gun fire which had killed several of their men.*
>
> *In all VC stunts the conditions are as important as the deed itself, and this deed was on all fours with many a pre-war VC.*

Division was determined that Longueval should be taken as soon as possible – preferably before. Therefore 11/Royal Scots, the 1st South African Infantry and 6/KOSB were ordered to launch another attack at 2 am on the 17th. The biggest failing in the attack was the bombardment, which was only of one hour's duration instead of two and a half hours (the reduction in time was due to the delay in withdrawing the forward infantry to safety) and the fact that the bombardment was unobserved, an extraordinary omission.

The night was pouring with rain, and it seems the Germans did not expect another attack at that stage. 11/Royal Scots advanced up on the left hand side, the KOSB on the right, including the east side of North Street. The conditions were atrocious, in sopping weather and pitch darkness, much of the fighting being with the bayonet. The darkness meant that many small groups of Germans were passed over and were thus able to attack from the rear, and so the Scots were drastically reduced in number. Amongst the early casualties was Captain BH Whitley, commanding A Company. It says something for the determination of his men that they were able to bring his body back from this exposed position, and he is now buried in Quarry Cemetery (I.E.4).

The British had pushed their way into the German defences, but were in reality surrounded by the enemy. The Germans launched a counter-attack under the light of Very flares, and the men were forced to retire to their position in Clarges Street.

6/KOSB had spent the first days of the battle serving as carriers of

Men from 26 Brigade, 9th Division returning from the trenches with an 8th Black Watch piper after the attack on Longueval.

trench and fighting stores for the other three battalions in the Brigade. This task had already cost them considerable casualties, and the almost hopeless task given to them only increased these. The regimental history confines itself to a few lines emphasising the impossibility of the set task. The only officer whose remains were subsequently identified was Second Lieutenant WJ Dunn, who is buried in AIF Cemetery. Almost certainly his body was recovered in the post-war clear-up of the battlefields.

Croft comments on these latter attacks,

I always thought that we were too prone to fight for each square yard instead of waiting till we were absolutely ready, involving fresh troops, and then going for the acres. It is not a bit of good asking stale troops to come with a wet sail.

This was the last major attack involving the men of the Brigade, and during the night of the 19th it was withdrawn to the relative safety of the Talus Boise, not far from Carnoy. Out of a total of some 3000 men, the Brigade lost 81 officers and 2033 men; the great majority of the killed and missing left their bones in the blood-soaked undergrowth of the orchards at Longueval.

26 (Highland) Brigade: pm 14 July – 19 July

Although much had gone right for 26 Brigade, there were two outstanding problems that it faced on 14 July; the German strongpoint at the south east of Longueval, and the tough nut of Waterlot Farm, the large sugar refinery on the Guillemont road.

7/Seaforths were tasked with capturing Waterlot Farm. The commanding officer, Lieutenant Colonel Kennedy anticipated that a German defensive barrage would fall on Montauban Alley, and therefore followed as close on the heels of 8/Black Watch as possible. His action was wise, and all but one of his platoons escaped the

Waterlot Farm before the war reached Longueval; in the early stages of the bombardment; and the site today. The refinery was demolished in the early 1990s.

hurricane of fire that the Germans laid down.

The War Diary provides background to the attack, not least the preparation and equipment before the attack.

On 2 and 3 July the battalion was in bivouac at Grove Town, a support area off the Fricourt to Bray road. On 4 July,

> *The bivouac was swamped by heavy thunderstorm in afternoon – 200 new shirts procured from stores to replace wettest – orders received for Battalion to proceed to billets in Billon Wood* [to the west of the farm of that name, south of Carnoy, off the Maricourt Road]. *8.30 pm Battalion marched off through mud to Billon Wood, leaving Quartermaster, transport officer and 15 spare officers with the first line transport in Grove Town. New Lewis gun handcarts could not cope with muddy roads.* [Croft was particularly scathing about the uselessness of the small wheels, and this so-called aid was soon abandoned from general use.]
>
> *5 July. Battalion remained in Billon Wood where there are good dugouts for most of the men.*

Here they stayed until 8 July, though casualties were suffered by a working party serving with the Royal Field Artillery, and it was still thought possible to despatch an officer (one of the reserve pool) to go to an Army Training School.

> *8 July. 5pm Battalion moved from Billon Wood valley to the trenches just NE of Carnoy village – 2 Coys in former No Man's Land and 2 Coys in original British trenches – Argylls in front of Battalion hold new front line.*
>
> *Battalion equipped as when marching from Vaux sur Somme, whence packs were sent to Corbie to be stored with guard of one man – viz – waterproof sheet under flap of haversack, greatcoats rolled, 2 smoke helmets, steel helmet, 2 mills bombs per man in pockets & 220 rounds SAA – (bombs and extra ammunition issued in Grove Town) haversack worn on back, with yellow patch sewn on, & Coys have a coloured patch on each shoulder in addition (red, yellow, dark blue and light blue).*

The Battalion stayed at Carnoy for a couple of days, providing assistance to the RE and suffering a trickle of casualties, including three officers wounded. On 10 July the Battalion strength is reported in the diary,

> *Strength with Battalion in the trenches: 19 Officers and 797 OR; Transport 1 Officer and 52 OR; with Transport 13 Officers and 69 OR; with Brigade HQ 1 Officer; with trench mortar*

carrying party & bombers 2 Officers and 45 OR; on command 6
Officers and 82 OR – total 42 Officers and 1045 OR.

At 7.30 pm the Battalion took over the front line from the Black Watch.

2 Coys holding Montauban Alley from s.22.c.7.2 to NE corner
of Bernafay Wood and 2 Coys in support near Train Alley.
Company in Bernafay Wood heavily shelled at night. Camerons
holding Montauban village, Black Watch and Argylls in reserve.
South Africans holding Montauban Alley on our right towards
Trônes Wood.

See Trench map page 131

For the next few days the Battalion remained in the line under heavy
artillery fire, suffering casualties amongst men (almost all wounded)
and support vehicles, such as a water cart and cooker. At 3 pm on the
13th the Company Commanders received their orders, verbally, with
the Battalion objective defined as Waterlot Farm via Longueval.

14 July. By 1.30 am the 2 coys from Train Alley (A and B) had
arrived in Montauban Alley, and the 8/Black Watch and
10/Argylls were forming up in front of the trenches. At 2.15 am C
and D coys commenced to leave the trenches and formed up
behind 8/Black Watch and 10/Argylls. During this time our guns
were shelling the Longueval position fairly heavily, and at Zero,
3.25 am the bombardment became intense for 5 minutes and then
the 26th Brigade advanced on Longueval with 8/Black Watch on

**British RAMC dresser tending a wounded German near Carnoy, 30th
July 1916.**

the right, the 10/Argylls on the left and the 7/Seaforths in support. 5/Camerons were in reserve just south of Montauban. The Brigade reached its first objective, the German trenches in front of Longueval, at about 3.45 am with slight casualties, but was held up there by enemy strong points, which consisted as a rule of a house containing 2 or 3 machine-gunners and about 10 bombers. The Brigade continued to consolidate the German trenches at about 4.30 am and continued under very heavy shell fire from all calibres of German guns.

At about 12 noon the 5/Camerons and the South African Infantry Brigade came up with orders to clear the northern portion of Longueval and Delville Wood, and an attack was made by D Coy of this Battalion on the strong point which was barring the way to Waterlot Farm. The strong point fell and our bombers commenced to work down to Waterlot Farm which they could not take as it was being fired on both by our heavy artillery and that of the enemy, however the trench was blocked near the farm and our men commenced the consolidation. Rations arrived at about 12 midnight. Six officers joined the Battalion. During the night the situation was fairly quiet with some shelling.[4]

Casualties of the Battalion on 14 July were 2 officers killed (one was the medical officer) and 11 wounded, with 250 OR killed and wounded. The two officers are commemorated on the Thiepval Memorial, as are most of the dead ORs.

At midnight the position of 26 Brigade was as follows: 10/Argylls held all the south and south-west of Longueval, with lines established in Clarges Street, Sloane Street and the old German front line from the Windmill to Pall Mall; 8/Black Watch were in a semi-circle around the north-east corner of the central square and also occupied a line 300 yards long parallel to and fifty yards south of Princes Street; three companies of 7/Seaforths held the old German line on the right of the 10/Argylls and the remaining company and three companies of 5/Camerons were in Longueval Alley as far as Trônes Wood, just west of Waterlot Farm.

The Divisional commander met the three brigadier-generals in Montauban and decided that the South African Brigade would attack Delville Wood at 5 am; if 27 Brigade failed to complete the capture of Longueval, the attack was to be launched from the south-west.

On 15 July two platoons of 5/Camerons, supported by two companies of the 4th South African Infantry attacked Waterlot Farm and managed to get through to the trenches beyond it, to the east, by noon. 4/South African Infantry attempted to consolidate these, but the enemy artillery made it impossible to hold the new trenches, so it was determined that it would be denied to the enemy by covering approaches to the farm with machine-guns from 26 Brigade and the South African Brigade in Delville Wood.

Meanwhile 7/Seaforths had maintained the pressure.

Patrols were sent out in the morning about Waterlot Farm and unfortunately Captain RWB McJannet was shot by the enemy in trying to take them prisoner. Nothing of note took place on this day except the intermittent bombardment of our newly won positions. Our rations arrived safely at about 11 pm and the watercarts which were brought up were emptied on to the road [this must have irritated the drivers more than somewhat, given the harrowing trip up the line that they must have endured!] *for the water supply was plentiful as a large supply of German mineral water was found in the village and much appreciated by all ranks. By this time the supply of grenades and SAA was most satisfactory as there was a large advanced Brigade dump just south of Longueval on the Montauban Longueval road, from which the Battalion dump was kept filled. Casualties for 15 July were 21 killed and wounded of all ranks.*

7/Seaforths were suffering stress and exhaustion by the 17th, but they were forced into the desperate defence of Delville Wood caused by the German counter-attack on 18 July. This will be discussed in the next chapter. The relief of the Battalion began on that evening when three companies of Bantams (men under the official height to join the army,

See annotated picture on page 36

A view to the east and north east showing the German front line 14 July 1916, and the area of heavy fighting throughout the second half of July and all of August.

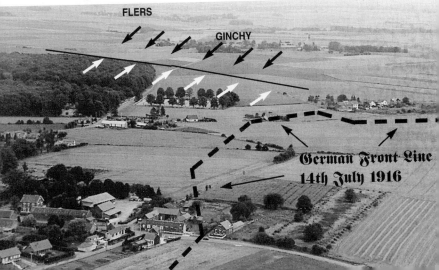

but then enlisted as special so-called 'Bantam' battalions) came up to the line and was completed the following morning. The Battalion suffered 22 officer casualties and 429 other ranks, of whom about ninety were killed. They marched out of the battle area to Sand Pit valley, to the south-east of Meaulte, where they joined the rest of the Brigade for a couple of days for rest and reorganisation.

Waterlot Farm was eventually captured on 17 July. At 9 am on 17 July, after a preliminary artillery bombardment, 'the Camerons, supported by two companies of 4/South African Infantry rushed the farm, slaughtered the garrison, and proceeded to consolidate the buildings'. It seems to me that prisoners were not an option for 5/Camerons, presumably enraged by the casualties that the brave German defenders had inflicted over the previous days and nights.

The part played by the Brigade in the defence of Delville Wood and its epic charge on 18 July is covered in the next chapter.

1. J Ewing, *The History of the 9th (Scottish) Division*. John Murray (London), 1921 p. 115
2. Ibid., pp 116 -117
3. Extracts and information for this section have been taken from the following:
Lieutenant Colonel WD Croft, *Three Years With the 9th (Scottish) Division,* John Murray, 1919
Major J Ewing, *The Royal Scots 1914 – 1919.* Edinburgh, 1925
Captain Stair Gillon, *The KOSB in the Great War.* Thomas Nelson and Sons, 1930.
4. Extracted from the War Diary of 7/Seaforth Highlanders, courtesy of the Regimental Museum.

Eighth Battalion, Black Watch, drawing the rum ration after their attack on Longueval, July 1916.

Chapter Three

THE SOUTH AFRICANS IN LONGUEVAL AND DELVILLE WOOD

(The clearest map for this chapter is on page 112)

The South African Brigade took over trenches on the Western Front for the first time on 6 May 1916, replacing 28 Brigade in the 9th Division. This Brigade had to be broken up because of a temporary manpower shortage caused by the limitations of the voluntary system that was the unique characteristic of the British army for the first eighteen months or so of the war. Most of the men had seen service in Egypt before coming to France. The great majority of them were of Anglo-Saxon origin, although about fifteen percent were of Afrikaner background. One battalion, 4/South African Regiment, wore the Atholl tartan.

For the attack on 14 July the Brigade was in reserve, which meant that over the next few days it was called in piecemeal to assist in resolving local difficulties that other brigades might have encountered and which were beyond their capability to resolve. This means that the South African Brigade was actually involved on most of the battle line that fell to the lot of the 9th Division, with the exception of the left flank.

The first members of the Brigade to be involved in the attack were 1/South African Regiment under the command of Lieutenant Colonel FS Dawson. His men were brought up to assist with the clearance of the northern part of Longueval, which had stubbornly held out against the best endeavours of 11 and 12/Royal Scots. The preliminary bombardment, which was scheduled to last for two hours, was restricted by the belief that members of the Royal Scots were already in parts of the village that were to be attacked, so for the most part it fell on the western part of the wood.

What followed afterwards is far from clear, almost inevitable given the nature of the ground over which the fighting took place. Street fighting is, notoriously, one of the most difficult forms of

Major-Gen Sir Henry Timson Lukin. Commanding South African Brigade to December 1916, and 9th Division from December 1916 to February 1918.

57

warfare, and a type for which, perhaps understandably, the army was not trained. It inevitably degenerates into small group actions and close quarter fighting; it is quite easy to pass over enemy positions, so that they can resume the fight once the initial sweep has gone over them; and it lends itself to what is laughingly known as 'friendly fire' casualties. Along with a night attack, it is one of the most difficult operations to control. Thus 1/South African Regiment split into small groups, with no one having a clear idea of what was happening. The first clear indication of the position of the men eventually got through to headquarters at 10.44 pm – ie almost nine hours after the attack was launched. At that stage there was a company in Piccadilly, immediately to the south of Duke Street; another was trying to work around from Piccadilly to North Street; nothing was known for certain of one company, believed to be on the east side of North Street; whilst one company was in reserve at the south east corner of the village.

Brigadier-General Scrase-Dickins, commanding 27 Brigade, instructed 1/South African Regiment to continue to work at clearing the village, which he wanted to be achieved by dawn; for the rest of the South African Brigade were due to launch their attack on Delville Wood from there at dawn on the 15th.

In the early hours of 15 July, before dawn, the South African Brigade, minus 1/South African Regiment, still involved in the fighting in Longueval, and two companies of 4/South African Regiment, involved in the fight for Waterlot Farm, moved up from Montauban to prepare for their attack on Delville Wood, taking up positions in trenches in the south-west corner of the wood. Command of the attack fell on the shoulders of Lieutenant Colonel WEC Tanner.

At first all went very well: the whole of the wood south of Princes Street was cleared by 7 am, and 138 prisoners were captured. Thus far, so good. However the next task was to clear the rest of the wood, towards the strong German positions in Longueval. The ground falls away as the village is approached, and the Germans were securely installed in their fortified houses and cellars.

Tanner instructed three companies of 2/South African Regiment to clear the wood from the east and to move forward as far as the Strand.

58

Lieutenant Colonel WEC Tanner.

At this point it is worth commenting on the 'streets' that run through Delville Wood. These were all given names of well known streets in London or Edinburgh. The great, wide, grass-covered boulevards that exist today, complete with their grand markers seem to be appropriately named Bond Street, Regent Street, the Strand, Princes Street and the like. At the time these were much, much narrower – perhaps a quarter or less of their present width. They existed for a number of reasons – to allow access to the wood for maintenance and clearing; as rides for horsemen, and as clear areas for those engaged in hunting. Similar rides exist in the other great woods of the Somme battlefield – and for similar purposes to those of pre-1914.

2/South African Regiment found the resistance of the enemy at this stage to be slight. In part this would have been because the Germans wished to minimise the casualties to their own men from the British artillery; in part because they had their hands full in the village itself and Waterlot Farm; in part because they had been caught off-balance by the earlier British success; and in part because they had a defence scheme for the wood that would not be revealed until the wood was almost entirely in British hands.

In any case, the Germans were not the main problem that 2/South African Regiment faced.

> *The profligate undergrowth and the tangle of trees and branches brought down by artillery fire rendered the laborious work of penetrating it most exhausting. When at length the perspiring and breathless South Africans reached the margin, the enemy's artillery opened a fierce bombardment on the whole place, and rifle and machine-gun fire prevented progress beyond the perimeter.*[1]

Thus Tanner could report, at 2 pm, that the wood, with the exception of the north west corner, was captured. But, in a real sense, the Brigade

An aerial view across the eastern part of the battlefield of 14 July 1916 and the subsequent weeks and months.

was in a trap. Instead of holding the wood with mini garrisons armed with machine-guns, who could provide mutual fire support, and with a centralised reserve to deal with enemy counter-attacks, it had to be fully and strongly held.

The wood was 159 acres in extent, and part of it was held by the enemy. Moreover, the Germans were exceptionally well situated for a counter-attack. They were able to direct an accurate fire on the wood from their batteries in the north, east

British artillery Forward Observation Officer amid the ruins of Longueval Church 17 July 1916. The shattered tree stumps of Delville Wood can be seen in the background. The day this photograph was taken the South African Brigade had a foothold in Delville Wood and were beating off repeated German counter-attacks.

and south-east. [One has only to see the view over the wood from the New Zealand memorial, off the Flers road, to appreciate the extent of an artillery observer's view over Delville Wood.] *Their trenches lay round its perimeter for much of its extent and commanded all its approaches; and the possession of Longueval ensured them a covered approach whenever they chose to deliver their stroke. Under these circumstances a strong garrison and constant vigilance were essential.*

Thus the German defence plan can be summarised; the wood was an easily identifiable target for its artillery. The British position was a salient into the German line at this point, particularly vulnerable whilst Guillemont remained in German hands. There was a relatively straightforward and secure means of gaining access to the wood whilst Longueval, the tunnel systems under and around it, the high ground around and to the south-east of High Wood and the valleys between the wood and Flers and Ginchy remained in German control. In other words, the situation could be controlled, and considerable casualties could be inflicted upon anyone defending the wood.

The South African Brigade set about setting up posts on the perimeter of the wood, and then faced the task of digging themselves in.

A plentiful supply of tools had been carried up by the South Africans and it was impressed upon the men that notwithstanding their weariness there could be no rest until trenches had been dug. But they had grasped the situation; it was only too obvious that their lives depended upon the speed with which they could dig themselves in. But the spendthrift undergrowth and tangled roots that crawled profusely in the soil of Delville Wood were hard to cut, and while the men toiled they were harried unceasingly by shell and machine-gun fire. An attempt to wire the edge of the wood was frustrated by a counter-attack, which men of the 10th Bavarian Division delivered, against the north-east corner about 3 pm. This attack was easily repulsed by rifle fire, but the situation was critical, and between 12.45 pm and 1.15 pm reports from 26 Brigade and 53 Brigade RFA having stated that the Germans were massing on the north-west of the wood, the artillery put a protective barrage round it.

The Germans were beaten off by 2/South African Regiment by 4.40 pm; but the South Africans had suffered considerable casualties from the heavy shell fire.

Overnight the defences of the wood were strengthened, the South

Africans assisted by the pioneer battalion, 9/Seaforths (more about the work of these undervalued men follows in a short chapter). Large stores of ammunition and grenades were also brought up, in anticipation of a hard struggle ahead. Most of the Brigade took up position around the perimeter – six companies on the line of the wood, three as a reserve. The western part of Princes Street was held by a half company of 2/South African Regiment and two companies of 1/South African Regiment guarded the flank from an attack from the village. Colonel Tanner's headquarters were close to the junction of Buchanan Street and Princes Street – as clearly marked by a stone obelisk in the wood today.

Meanwhile the troops of 4/South African Regiment had been engaged in the battle for Waterlot Farm, as described in the earlier chapter.

By the night of 15 July the Division was in an exhausted state – engaged in heavy fighting in Longueval, Delville Wood and Waterlot Farm, with not a fresh battalion remaining to the GOC, Major-General Furse. Meanwhile the Germans had been reorganising themselves in the light of the relatively successful British attack. This meant the pumping in of massive reinforcements to hold Longueval and Delville Wood – the holding of either of which was the key to unravelling the whole position. If the British captured Delville Wood, then Longueval would fall – and similarly Delville Wood would fall if Longueval was taken.

Furse had fallen out with the Corps Commander (Congreve) and his artillery adviser. Furse wanted heavy artillery to destroy the enemy

The inscription reads: *Here in a shallow trench stood the battle headquarters of the South African Infantry during the fighting in Delville Wood.* **Paths and trenches to the rear lead to the west and south west of the wood.**

positions in Longueval, but this was not under his command. His seniors had insisted that the position should be taken as soon as possible, and this precluded the time necessary to withdraw the infantry and prepare an artillery plan (and divert the necessary resources) for such an action. Therefore Furse had to accept the need to continue by means of infantry attack and his own limited artillery resources.

The solution was an attack simultaneously on the village and the north-western part of the wood to be launched at 10 am on 16 July, preceded by a bombardment with 2 inch trench mortars (Croft's 'half dumb bells'). 1/South African Regiment would provide two companies for the attack, which failed. However, it was the occasion of a VC action.

Private WF Faulds VC

His VC was gazetted on 9 September 1916.

A bombing party under Lieutenant Craig attempted to rush over 40 yards of ground which lay between the British and German trenches. Coming under very heavy rifle and machine-gun fire the officer and the majority of the party were killed or wounded. Unable to move, Lieutenant Craig lay midway between the two lines of trenches, the ground being quite open. In full daylight Private Faulds, accompanied by two other men, climbed over the parapet, ran out, picked up the officer, and carried him back, one man being severely wounded in so doing. Two days later Private Faulds again showed most conspicuous bravery in going out alone to bring in a wounded man, and carrying him nearly half a mile to a dressing station, subsequently rejoining his platoon. The artillery fire at the time was so intense that stretcher-bearers and others considered that any attempt to bring in the wounded man meant certain death. This risk Private Faulds faced unflinchingly, and his bravery was crowned with success.

Faulds was commissioned in May 1917, but was wounded and captured by the Germans in their spring offensive in March 1918. After the war he moved to Salisbury in Rhodesia, where he died in August 1950, at the age of 55.

16 July was a period of consolidation, where practicable, for the British and for harassment by the Germans, in particular from brave and persistent snipers, accompanied by an unrelenting artillery bombardment, which continued to take a heavy toll of the defenders of Delville Wood. Communications within the wood, by runner, between the scattered perimeter posts was extremely difficult, and the men were perpetually on edge. Rest was quite impracticable. Brigadier-General HT Lukin, the Brigade commander, tried in vain to get his men relieved – but, to be fair, Furse had no one else to send in to relieve the South Africans. Furse now asked once more for heavy artillery to be used, with observed fire, to pound the German defences in the northern part of Longueval. This was agreed in principle, which would allow an attack at 4 am on 17 July. But Fourth Army commander, Rawlinson, insisted that the attack be launched earlier and the village taken before dawn. The consequences of this have been discussed in the section on 27 Brigade, and as already explained, the attack failed.

Furse did get, however, some relatively fresh troops, as 76 Brigade (part of the 3rd Division) came under his command to replace the shattered remnant of 27 Brigade.

17 July passed much as the preceding day – the South Africans again coming under persistent shelling during the night of the 16th, and dreading the full onslaught of German counter-attacks in force. In the evening of 17 July Lieutenant Colonel Tanner was wounded and Lieutenant Colonel Thackeray took his place. Furse also intended to relieve the other two brigades, but these decided to stay put in the light of the attack by new troops.

The Germans now added to the misery of the defenders by firing 'thousands of gas shells into the battery positions and back areas', causing confusion to the British artillery support. This was accompanied by a number of assaults against the defensive perimeter of the wood, most notably one from the north west in which the enemy got as far as the junction between Buchanan Street and Princes Street; however all the attacks broke down.

The attack of 76 Brigade, launched at 3.45 am on 18 July, did well (as was by now becoming customary with such British attacks), but the Germans still held out in some isolated posts, enough to provide the basis for their next attack.

The German counter attack of 18 July.

A massive German bombardment opened up at 8 am which continued without let-up until 7 pm. The divisional historian considers that this 'was probably the heaviest the Division ever experienced'. It was almost inevitable that communications were severely disrupted, with no one aware of what the situation of the South Africans in the wood might be. By 2 pm there was an increase in the tempo of the shelling so that trenches (and often their occupants) were obliterated. At this time the Germans launched their attack and

The SOS signal was seen in the wood and the village, and some of our men were noticed dribbling back from these places. Practically all the South Africans on the perimeter had perished, and the few survivors, stupefied by the ferocity of the shelling, fell back on Lieutenant Colonel Thackeray's HQ in Princes Street. At 3 pm waves of Germans poured through the wood and the northern part of Longueval, but now seizing their opportunity our machine-gunners took heavy toll of the men in field-grey. The troops performed prodigies of valour, and in a sustained and delirious struggle the heroic defenders baffled every effort of the foe to break their ranks. In this grisly combat the Germans lost much valuable time, and when they pressed on, the gallant South Africans were still holding out.

Private JA Lawson, 3/South African Regiment, described the events of that day – events which transformed the 1500 or so defenders that were in position on the morning of 18 July to 143 when they staggered out of the wood a couple of days later – and there had been South African reinforcements in between times.

Lieutenant Colonel Thackeray

Our little party had to wait in their cramped position of tortured suspense till nearly 3 pm for the only relief we now looked for – the relief afforded by the excitement of desperate fighting against great odds. The enemy now launched an attack in overwhelming numbers, amid the continued roar of artillery. Once more they found us ready – a small party of utterly worn-out men, shaking off their sleep to stand up in the shallow trench. As the Huns came on they were mowed down – every shot must have told. Our rifles smoked and became unbearably hot; but though the end seemed near, it was not yet. When the Huns wavered and broke, they were reinforced and came on again. We again prevailed and drove them back. Only one Hun crossed our trench, to be shot in the heart a few yards behind it. The lip of our trench told more plainly than I can how near they were to not failing. Beyond, in No Man's Land, we could do something to estimate the cost of their failure. Exhaustion now did what shell fire and counter-attacks had failed to do, and we collapsed in our trench, spent in body and at last worn out in spirit. The task we had been set was too great for us. What happened during the next two hours or so I do not know. Numbed in all my senses, I gazed vacantly into space, feeling as if the whole thing had been a ghastly nightmare, out of which I was now only waiting complete deliverance. From this state of coma I was awakened

The defence of Delville Wood by the South Africans.

by a shell which exploded just over me, and instantaneously I passed into unconsciousness. When I regained consciousness a few minutes after, my first sensation was that of having been thoroughly refreshed by sleep, But on moving I found that the fight for me was over... I tried to rouse my friend, who had fallen face downward beside me. Getting no response, I lifted his head, calling upon him by name, but I could not arouse him. I then began with pain and difficulty to walk down the line. I found that the last two hours of shelling had done their work – only six remained alive in the trench. I aroused one sleeper, and told him I had been badly hit, and was going to try and walk out. He faced me for a second, and asked me what to do. I said there was nothing to do but carry on, as the orders of Saturday morning had not been countermanded. His brave 'Right-O!' were the last words I heard there – surely fitting words as the curtain fell for me.

Furse, in Montauban, ordered 10/Argylls to recapture all the ground north and west of Regent Street, but they found it impossible to penetrate the barrage falling along the line of Clarges Street. At 33.30 pm Lieutenant Colonel Dawson was told off to collect the men of 1st and 4th South African Regiment and take them up to the Strand and the northern boundary of the wood. He managed to assemble 160 men – effectively an understrength company – and set off for the wood at 4

Looking south west over Delville Wood and the area over which the British attacked on the 14th July 1916.

Looking south west over Delville Wood and the area over which the British attacked on the 14th July 1916.

pm. Drawing close to the position he was told by a number of officers that the garrison had ceased to exist, and so he left his men in old German trenches to the south west of the village and went forward himself to see what was going on. A number of men went past him in confusion, but he discovered that remnants of the South Africans were still holding out in Buchanan Street, and so he took his men and put them in trenches to the north of Dover Street and in contact with 26/Brigade on the right. By 6 pm all Longueval north of Clarges Street had been lost, with the exception of a few posts held by members of the Highland Brigade; whilst only a tiny part of Delville Wood remained in British hands – that held by Lieutenant Colonel Thackeray in Princes Street and 5/Camerons lining Buchanan Street.

Lieutenant Colonel Gordon of the Black Watch decided that the time was now ripe for a counter-attack – despite the fact that the troops of the Highland Brigade had spent most of the day cowering into the sides of their trenches, south of Clarges Street, whilst bedlam went on all around them. He agreed with Lieutenant Colonel Kennedy of 7/Seaforths on a plan of action. All available men were lined up in trenches which ran north of the spur of the railway line that ran in to Longueval from Guillemont. They charged towards Delville Wood; meanwhile Lieutenant Colonel Duff led his men in Buchanan Street westwards, towards the village. Having crossed the square of Longueval, 26 Brigade was suddenly confronted with the sight of hordes of Germans pouring out of the south-west corner of the wood.

For all who took part in that attack this was the most thrilling moment of the war. For the space of a single second both sides hesitated, so dramatic was the meeting, and then from the left of the 26th line came the rousing command, 'Forward Boys!' and the Highlanders surged on like an irresistible wave. The Germans wavered, fired a few shots, and bolted into the shelter of Delville, refusing to face a force that was less than a quarter of their strength. Carried away by the impetuosity of this magnificent charge, many of the Highlanders heedlessly followed the enemy far into the thicket, where many a brave man, marked on the casualty lists as 'missing', met his fate in a lonely scuffle with the Germans.

It was fortunate that Kennedy and Gordon were able to regain control of the bulk of their men before the charge was transformed into a headlong rush into disaster. One machine-gun had been missed in the attack and was already causing casualties, and the group was in danger of being outflanked. 5/Camerons fell back on Buchanan Street, minus the guiding hand of their CO, Lieutenant Colonel Duff, who had been severely wounded; the rest returned to Clarges Street and the trench north of the church; whilst the support line was in the original jumping-off trench. The situation had been restored in Longueval, at least to the extent that the British retained a firm grip on the southern part of it, but the same could not be said of Delville Wood.

Some 80 men of the Trench Mortar Company, sent in by Lieutenant Colonel Dawson, had reinforced the South Africans in the wood. But matters still looked desperate, no more so than around the headquarters of the Brigade, where the wounded and dying were piling up with no hope of getting them away to the relative safety of the Advanced Dressing Station, situated at Glatz Redoubt, to the south-east of Montauban. Lieutenant Colonel Dawson made his way into the wood at about midnight to help where he could; but matters were not helped when 5/Camerons were moved to reinforce he Clarges Street line during the night, leaving the whole defence of the wood to the South Africans. The Germans attacked three times during the night, each time fended off by the thinning line of South Africans defenders.

Furse was now given 53 Brigade under command, and resolved to counter-attack. From 7.30 pm it was possible to lay a barrage east of Buchanan Street and north of Princes Street, there no longer being any British defenders there. 19/DLI of

Lieutenant Colonel Dawson,

53 Brigade was ordered to clear the wood south of Princes Street at 12.30 am on 19 July, but this was an unrealistic proposal, given the amount of time they had to get themselves in position, the darkness, their complete ignorance of the position and the heavy shelling. In the event, these bantams were not called upon to attack, but spent their time in support of 26 Brigade and providing an escort for prisoners. 53 Brigade went on to clear the wood south of Princes Street at 7.30 am, but for some unexplained reason, did not relieve, as ordered, the South Africans.

All of the South African Brigade had been relieved on the night of the 18th, except for the defenders of the wood, and withdrew to Happy Valley; Lieutenant Colonel Thackeray's force did not finally join them until 21 July, having been relieved during the evening of 20 July.

Thackeray was joined by two wounded officers and 140 men.

It does not seem out of place, amidst all the killing and slaughter, to reproduce a personal account of an anonymous stretcher-bearer in the South African Field Ambulance. Spellings of place names have been corrected, as well as errors of fact about the battle.

As the casualties were exceedingly numerous, we had our work cut out in collecting and carrying the wounded to the dressing stations, which we had established in the captured German trenches, in their capacious and extremely useful dugouts. I did not go up to the line until the 14th. I had not been up at our advance dressing station, known as Glatz Redoubt, more than a couple of hours when a small piece of shrapnel hit me in the muscle of the right arm. Owing, however, to my shirt sleeve being rolled, the force of the piece was broken, and I escaped with a slight puncture, about half an inch deep, and a deep bruise, both of which are quite better now. Owing to this I was unable to carry stretchers that evening, but pushed a trolley up and down the light railway (formerly German) which lay between Montauban and Carnoy, a distance of about two and a half miles. By means of this trolley we took a large number of stretcher cases down to the latter place.

The following night myself and three other bearers were despatched for duty up the line. We came under a fairly heavy bombardment during the night, one of our party sustaining shell-shock, which necessitated his removal to the dressing station. The three of us were kept extremely busy, and were not relieved until we had been carrying patients for 27 solid hours, each journey – from Longueval to Bernafay Wood, being a distance of about a mile. What food we had consisted of bits of biscuits which we found lying alongside dead bodies; and we never had a single rest during that time.

We did not have to go on duty again until the morning of the 17th, as the RAMC had relieved us. We proceeded to Bernafay Wood, which was under an extremely heavy shell fire, and owing to this we could not go up to Longueval to fetch the wounded. As the fire had not abated by about 6 pm our officer decided to go up, as there were a large number of cases waiting to be removed from the village. Accordingly we started off, four men to a stretcher, at a distance of about 20 yards apart. We had not gone more than half a mile when ten of our bearers were knocked over and had to be taken back to the wood. We then went back up again (about 24 of us in all), and reached the village in safety, though we had some very narrow escapes on the way. It was a horrible job removing the patients, as the roads were one mass of shell craters at a distance of about 2 feet apart; and as it had been raining on and off for nearly five days these were mostly half-full of water, and we were constantly falling into them, patient and all. Our greatcoats and equipment we had disposed of long before, and we were all wet through to the skin. We were knocked down twice owing to the concussion of shells bursting quite near us, and it was a miracle that we were not all blown to pieces. Three trips we managed safely, but on the fourth a shell burst very close to us – we were carrying the stretcher on our shoulders, one man to each handle – and we were all flung down. The patient was killed, the three other bearers wounded, while I escaped with a piece of shrapnel through my coat and my steel

Captured Germans look on as the RAMC carry a wounded soldier to a dressing station, taken near Bernafay Wood.

helmet being knocked off. I patched the other bearers up as best I could, and we managed to get safely down to the wood. It was about 2 am by now, and I was sent up to the village to see if I could be of any help. As I was nearing Longueval I saw a walking patient coming down, and when about twenty yards from me a shell burst almost exactly next to him. Seeing him fall I ran up and found that his left foot had been taken clean off, so I tied up the artery, and as there was nobody in sight to give me a hand I managed to get him on my back and started carrying him to the Scottish Regimental Aid Post [ie 4/South African Regiment], *which was about a hundred yards away. I had not gone more than ten yards when a big shell burst under me, and I was picked up and flung about ten feet away into a shell crater, landing on the side of my head. I just remember coming round again and starting to climb out, when I heard a terrific explosion, and the earth seemed to hit me in the face. When I came round again I had a splitting headache, and was bleeding from my nose, ear and mouth. The second shell had completely buried me, but luckily some Camerons saw me getting up, and they dug me out as quickly as possible. At first I thought part of my head had been blown off, but I found that everything was all right, with the exception of my one ear, which was quite deaf. On remembering my patient, we went to look for him, but found him smashed to pieces. They then helped me down to the wood, and as I was feeling pretty bad I was sent to hospital at Rouen* [one of the major Base Hospitals] *the following day.*

The anonymous medic was transferred to England, where he was taken to the South African hospital in Richmond. A former staff sergeant graphically describes the problems that the stretcher-bearers faced in the Field Ambulance.

The road from Longueval to Bernafay Wood [ie Pall Mall] *was in an indescribable condition. It was impossible to carry from the front to the RAP in Longueval, owing to the sniping, which was at times very severe and accurate. The rear was a mass of ruins, wire entanglements, garden fences, fallen and falling trees, together with every description of debris and shattered building material. It was one thing to clear a path along which the reinforcements may be brought, but quite another to make a track on which four men may carry a stretcher with a modicum of comfort to the patient... Besides this road there was a narrow sunken lane which at first afforded some safety, but later became*

> *so pitted with shell holes that the bearers had to take to the open. In addition to these difficulties, it must be remembered that these roads were shelled heavily day and night.*
>
> *One of the worst experiences of this shell fire was when it was decided to shell Longueval once more. Very short notice was given to clear all RAPs, and only two men per stretcher could be spared. Padres, doctors and odd men were pressed into service to enable all patients to be removed. As the party left, the bombardment began on both sides. Scrambling, pushing and slipping amid a tornado of shell fire, they headed for Bernafay Wood. It was impossible to keep together, and in the darkness squads became easily detached and lost touch. The noise of bursting shells was incessant and deafening, while the continuous sing of the rifle and machine-gun bullets overhead tried the nerves of the hardiest. To crown all, it was raining, and the roads were almost impassable for stretcher work. In fact, had it not been for the light of the German star shells, the thing could not have worked at all. As the night wore on squad after squad of tired, soaked and mud-covered men stumbled into Bernafay Wood. here came a medical officer covered with mud and grime from top to toe, carrying a stretcher with a kilted Scot. Then a tall parson, unrecognisable under a coating of mud, with a stretcher-bearer as partner, whose orders he obeyed implicitly.*

In one case the Medical Officer, found that it was impossible to move all his stretcher cases, and so remained behind in his post. Buchan quotes the Field Ambulance records.

> *The Aid Post was in a building, and as the Germans were counter-attacking and our troops going out, the windows and doors were barricaded with mattresses, furniture and anything that might stop a bullet. During the night dressing the wounded was carried out under great difficulty, as only a small electric torch or candle could be used. Rev E Hill, who had also remained to help, managed to keep up a constant supply of tea and coffee, apparently from supernatural sources.*

At midnight on 14 July the Brigade had 121 officers and 3032 men; the total that came together at Happy Valley was about 750. 1/South African Regiment suffered 558 casualties; the 2nd 482, the 3rd 771 and the 4th 509. 23 officers were killed, 7 died of wounds (most of these are buried at Corbie Communal Cemetery), 47 were wounded and 15 were prisoners or missing. All commissioned ranks of 2 and 3/South African Regiment and who were in the wood became casualties, as did all those of the Machine Gun Corps Company attached to the Brigade.

The Divisional historian looked back at the events of mid-July with pride.

The defence of Delville Wood by Lieutenant Colonel Thackeray's small band rightly takes its place as one of the classic feats of the war. But, though less well known, the charge of the Highlanders that saved Longueval when a serious disaster seemed inevitable, is an achievement that ought to secure a lasting place in our military annals. Not merely does it illustrate the unflinching courage of the Highlanders of the 26th Brigade, but it is a brilliant example of the value of a prompt counter-attack boldly carried out by even a few men against a resolute and numerous enemy.

The remains of Delville Wood after the battle had moved on. It is still possible to see the remains of roots and undergrowth which made digging trenches and shelters very difficult.

NOMINAL ROLL OF OFFICERS OF THE SOUTH AFRICAN INFANTRY BRIGADE—DELVILLE WOOD, JULY 1916.*

Brigadier-General H. T. LUKIN, C.B., C.M.G., D.S.O.
Major J. MITCHELL-BAKER, D.S.O.
Captain A. L. PEPPER.
Lieutenant F. R. ROSEBY . . . . Died of wounds.
Sec.-Lieutenant F. W. S. BURTON.

1ST REGIMENT.

Name and Rank.	Remarks.
Lieut.-Col. F. S. DAWSON, C.M.G. . .	
Major F. H. HEAL	With transport.
„ E. T. BURGES	Killed.
Captain G. J. MILLER	Killed.
„ H. H. JENKINS.	Wounded.
„ P. J. JOWETT	Missing (assumed dead).
Lieutenant T. O. PRIDAY (Adjutant). .	Wounded.
„ S. W. E. STYLE	Wounded.
„ C. B. PARSONS	Killed.
„ C. F. S. NICHOLSON . . .	
„ E. A. DAVIES	Transport Officer.
„ W. S. DENT	Wounded.
„ J. M. HOLLINGWORTH . .	Missing (assumed dead).
„ A. W. CRAIG	Wounded.
„ L. I. ISSACS	
„ H. G. CHAPMAN	Wounded.
„ F. S. ENGLISH	
„ A. C. HARRISON	Wounded.
„ W. D. HENRY	{ Wounded and missing (since prisoner of war).
„ W. A. LARMUTH	Wounded.
„ A. W. LEIFELDT	Wounded.
„ C. W. REID.	Wounded.
„ W. N. BROWN	Killed.
„ A. STUCKEY	
„ E. J. BURGESS	Wounded.
Sec.-Lieut. A. C. HAARHOFF . . .	

* The roll is exclusive of the Machine Gun Company, the Trench Mortar Battery, the Field Ambulance, and the 64th Field Company Royal Engineers, all of which took part in the battle.

Sec.-Lieut. A. E. BROWN	Killed.
„ E. A. L. HAHN	Killed.
„ W. TEMPANY	Wounded.
„ P. W. FURMIDGE . . .	Wounded.
„ C. I. BATE	Prisoner.
„ R. M. LYNE	
Q.M. and Hon. Captain A. C. WEARNER	
Attached.	
Chaplain and Captain E. St. C. HILL .	

2ND REGIMENT.

Name and Rank.	Reme
Lieut.-Col. W. E. TANNER, C.M.G. . .	Wounded.
Major H. H. GEE	Died of wou
Captain H. W. M. BAMFORD (Adjt.) .	Wounded.
„ C. R. HEENAN	Wounded.
„ E. BARLOW	Wounded.
„ H. E. CLIFFORD	Died of wou
„ W. F. HOPTROFF	Killed.
„ W. J. GRAY.	Killed.
Lieutenant H. E. F. CREED. . . .	Killed.
„ L. GREENE	Wounded.
„ W. J. HILL	Killed.
„ F. M. DAVIS	Wounded.
„ C. T. K. LETCHFORD . . .	Killed.
„ C. L. H. MULCAHY. . . .	Died of wou
„ R. BEVERLEY	Wounded.
„ W. J. PERKINS	Wounded.
Sec.-Lieut. T. W. BRU-DE-WOLD .	Killed.
„ E. V. TATHAM	Killed.
„ A. R. KNIBBS	Wounded.
„ R. G. MILLER	Killed.
„ B. N. MACFARLANE . . .	Wounded.
„ E. C. BRYANT	Injured.
„ R. P. TATHAM	Killed.
„ F. G. WALSH	Transport off
„ A. T. WALES	Killed.
„ G. GREEN	Wounded.
„ W. H. FLEMMER	Died of wou
„ N. FENIX	Wounded.

Sec.-Lieut. J. G. CONNOCK	Killed.
Q.M. and Hon. Captain E. A. LEGGE .	
Attached.	
Chaplain and Captain P. J. WALSHE .	

3RD REGIMENT.

Name and Rank.	Remarks.
Lieut.-Col. E. F. THACKERAY, C.M.G. .	Wounded. (At duty.)
Captain (Acting-Major) J. W. JACKSON	Killed.
„ R. F. C. MEDLICOTT . . .	Prisoner.
„ D. R. MACLACHLAN . . .	Killed.
„ E. V. VIVIAN	Wounded.
„ L. W. TOMLINSON	Wounded.
„ A. W. H. M'DONALD (Adjt.) .	Wounded.
Lieutenant O. H. de B. THOMAS . .	{ Wounded and missing (since prisoner of war).
„ J. B. BAKER	Wounded.
„ A. L. PAXTON	Wounded.
„ A. M. THOMSON	Wounded.
„ B. H. L. DOUGHERTY . . .	Wounded.
„ D. A. PIRIE.	Prisoner.
„ H. M. HIRTZEL	Prisoner.
„ H. G. ELLIOTT	Missing (assumed dead).
„ E. J. PHILLIPS	Wounded.
Sec.-Lieut. S. B. STOKES	Wounded.
„ D. JENNER	Wounded.
„ A. E. BARTON	Killed.
„ A. E. SHARPE	Gassed.
„ F. K. ST. M. RITCHIE . .	Prisoner.
„ D. M. ABEL.	Wounded.
„ H. W. GOVE	Missing (assumed dead).
„ C. H. DICK	Killed.
„ F. H. SOMMERSET . . .	Killed.
„ A. C. HANKS	Died of Wounds.
„ S. PEARSON	Wounded.
„ S. J. GUARD	Wounded and prisoner.
„ W. SCALLAN	Wounded.
„ H. N. HEELEY	Wounded.
„ D. J. W. GOWIE	Shell shock.
Q.M. and Hon. Lieut. W. H. CARDING .	

Attached.	
Captain S. LIEBSON, S.A.M.C . . .	Wounded.
Chaplain and Captain G. T. COOK . .	Killed.

4TH REGIMENT.

Name and Rank.	Remar
Lieut.-Col. F. A. JONES, C.M.G., D.S.O.	Killed.
Major D. M. MACLEOD	Wounded.
„ D. R. HUNT	
Captain E. C. D. GRADY	Wounded.
„ T. H. ROSS	
„ C. M. BROWNE (Adjutant) .	Wounded.
„ S. C. RUSSELL	Died of woun
„ W. ANDERSON	Shell shock.
„ G. E. W. MARSHALL . . .	Shell shock.
„ F. McE. MITCHELL . . .	Attached 26t
Lieutenant A. M. CAMERON	Wounded.
„ J. L. SHENTON	Wounded.
„ H. M. NEWSON. . . .	Prisoner.
„ T. FARRELL.	Gassed.
„ C. M. GUEST	Staff.
„ A. H. BROWN	Killed.
„ J. WATKINS	Wounded.
„ R. D. GRIERSON . . .	Gassed.
„ W. McLEAN	Brigade Staff.
„ A. S. TAYLOR	Wounded.
„ H. G. OUGHTERSON . .	Killed.
„ R. B. THORBURN . . .	Killed.
„ G. SMITH	Wounded.
„ A. V. CHASE	Wounded.
„ J. S. FRY	Killed.
„ A. YOUNG, V.C. . . .	Wounded.
Sec.-Lieut. C. S. BELL	Killed.
„ D. ROSS	Killed.
„ W. H. KIRBY	Wounded.
„ C. A. A. MACLEAN . . .	Wounded.
„ E. F. DALGETY	
Q.M. and Hon. Lieut. Z. B. BAYLY.	
Attached.	
Major M. B. POWER, S.A.M.C. . . .	
Chaplain and Captain S. THOMSON . .	

'Nancy' the 4th Regiment mascot. the springbok 'Nancy' was presented to the Regiment in August 1915 by Mr D M'Laren Kennedy of Driefontein, Orange Free State. She accompanied the 4th to Egypt, and thence to France, where she was with the Brigade in all its battles. She was wounded in 1917. She died at Hermeton, in Belgium, on 28th November 1918.

Lieutenant Colonel Tanner, of 2/South African Regiment, himself wounded during the battle, wrote in his report:

> *Each individual was firm in the knowledge of his confidence in his comrades, and was, therefore, able to fight with that power which good discipline alone can produce. A finer record of this spirit could not be found than the line of silent bodies along the Strand over which the enemy had not dared to tread.*

John Buchan ends his narrative of the battle by talking of their Brigadier's reaction.

> *But the most impressive tribute was that of their Brigadier. When the remnant of his Brigade paraded before him, Lukin took the salute with uncovered head and eyes not free from tears.*

---

1. *History of the 9th Division*, op cit, p.121. The divisional history is used as the basis of this chapter.
2. Extracted from J Buchan, *The History of the South African Forces in France*. Thomas Nelson n.d.

Also of value in this chapter has been *The Story of Delville Wood: Told in Letters from the Front*. This was a compendium of correspondence from the troops, mainly to family members and therefore censored, published in 1918, before the war had ended.

Chapter Four

THE UNSUNG HEROES: THE PIONEERS, 9th SEAFORTH HIGHLANDERS

The Pioneer battalion of the 9th Division since its arrival in France was 9/Seaforths. The job of the Pioneer battalions was to work in constructing field works and fortifications of various types – from strong points to wiring, from communication trenches to road repair and maintenance. During the battle in which the 9th Division fought in and around Longueval and Delville Wood, 9/Seaforths was split up amongst the attacking battalions: A Company was with 26 Brigade; B Company with the South African Brigade; C Company with 27 Brigade and D Company, in the immediate rear, making good and repairing, or building, tram ways and roads.

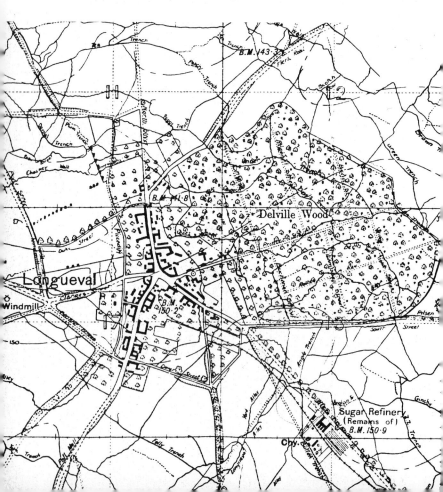

Trench maps are split into a series of squares, each given a designation of a letter. These are split into 36 smaller squares, given a number. Each of these squares in turn is subdivided into four, lettered a,b,c,d, starting from top left, top right, bottom left, bottom right. These are then subdivided into ten along both the horizontal and the upright, allowing for a fairly accurate placing of points on a map. These points are used by taking the horizontal divisions of ten first (the eastings), and then the vertical (the northings) – best remembered by thinking of 'bottoms up'

See also trench map on page 131

A Company.

This Company spent its time after the relatively successful attack in this area of the Somme battle on 1 July repairing roads (eg a track on the side of the Carnoy – Montauban railway) and making trenches effective once more after the heavy bombardment they had undergone (eg Silesia Alley). On 3 July it laid out barbed wire entanglements on the east side of Bernafay Wood.

Wiring in progress 30 yards from edge of wood when KOSBs

TAYLOR LIBRARY

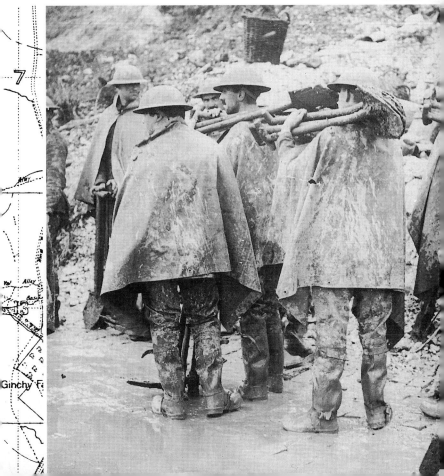

opened fire on Pioneers which much delayed work.

It also, doubtless, led to a free and frank exchange of views! The company continued working at the wiring until the early morning of 5 July before it was switched to making bridges on the track mentioned above and then spent three days (until 9 July) making the road between Carnoy and Montauban. In the days immediately before the battle the Company made four strong points to the north and east of Montauban, wired them and sapped out for dugouts and also reclaimed Breslau Alley.

At 7 am on the morning of 14 July the Company received orders from the Brigade

> *To proceed to Longueval and construct strong points at s.17.a.9.8; s.17.b,5.9; s.18.c.1.9 and to report to the CO Black Watch. Take up Company together with carrying party of 60 Camerons. Owing to heavy shell fire and absence of reliable information as to whether the positions were held by us or not, I sent up a patrol under Lieutenant Griffith who found that only one of the proposed sites was in our hands. I detailed No. 2 Platoon and they loopholed and wired the Centre Keep s.17.d.3.9, clearing entrance and consolidating. No. 3 Platoon (Lieutenant Walker) was detailed to dig out and wire a strong point on W side of Longueval, s.17.a.9.2 which was completed. I reported to CO Black Watch, and as he had no further work for remainder of Company I placed No 1 Platoon (Lieutenant Druitt) to dig and complete section of the communication trench. No 4 Platoon was sent back to Montauban Alley to await further instructions.*

Wiring parties going up to the front line after heavy rain.

At 5 am on the 15th Nos 1 and 2 platoons left Montauban Alley for Longueval.

> *No 2 (Lieutenant Griffith) working on Centre Keep, connecting cellars with dugouts and consolidating. No 1 proceeded to s.18.c.1.9, but were driven off by machine-gun fire at close range. Reported to Colonel Gordon and platoon was sent back. At 8 pm I took up Lieutenant Walker and Nos 3 and 4 Platoons and reported to Colonel Gordon, and as the proposed sites for strong points were still held by the enemy, we built a strong barricade at Cross Roads s.17.b.5.4.*

The men were back at work again by 7 am on the 16th, with No 1 Platoon deepening existing trenches at s.18.c.1.9., making machine-gun emplacements and sapping V slits. Meanwhile No 2 Platoon cut new trenches in Centre Keep and generally improved the defensive strength of the position by setting up wire entanglements and further consolidation. A decision to use some of the rest of the Company to work on a new trench for the Camerons was abandoned in the early afternoon when the decision was taken to withdraw men from the wire prior to the heavy bombardment before a further attack was made on the German positions. The 17th was spent in the vicinity of Montauban; the time there was made even more unpleasant by gas shells, which meant that gas helmets had to be worn for four hours.

The 18th proved to be very tough day. At 3am two Platoons (Nos 1 and 3) were ordered to follow up the advance of 1/South African Infantry and construct a strong point at s.11.d.5.3. They reported to the CO of 7/Seaforths who provided them with a covering party. This had later to be sent back because a message was received from 2/South African Infantry that 100 Gordons were in the orchard in front of their position and needed entrenching tools to be brought up. Lieutenant Walker reported to Colonel Thackeray that this would be done as soon as the strong point was started.

> *As soon as the South Africans advanced, the party followed up and commenced digging strong point. At 11 am numbers of the Gordons left the front edge of the wood and crowded into the trenches under construction, but in spite of the heavy shelling the work was proceeded with and nearly finished and only when the party was reduced to 12, and the covering party had retired owing to the intense bombardment, did Lieutenant Walker collect the wounded and arrive back in Montauban at 7.30 pm.*

Whilst No 3 Platoon had been having a torrid time under fire, No 1 Platoon had been engaged in carrying material for wiring. In our day and age when practically everything of any weight is transported by mechanical means it is difficult to imagine the difficulties of staggering along a shell blasted terrain, under continual shell and machine-gun fire, on occasion having to do this with the constrictions caused by wearing a gas helmet and at the same time having to wear equipment and carry a personal weapon. Around Longueval may be seen numbers of cork screw pickets used to hold barbed wire in place; they are doing the same job for farmers today. They are heavy and cumbersome. On occasion amongst the iron harvest may be found great coils of barbed wire, now rusted together in a reddish brown mass. These are just two of the items that these men would have been required to haul up to Longueval across the valley from Montauban. Despite the best endeavours, it was decided that it was impossible to continue wiring under the sustained shell fire; and in any case the wood was going to be evacuated for a further barrage.

One of the problems for the Pioneers was the matter of command. 9/Seaforths were scattered in several locations across the divisional area. Companies, in turn, were distributed amongst the brigades and platoons amongst the battalions. The consequence was that orders to platoons tended to come from a variety of sources, and this is one of the reasons why the War Diary entries are specific as to the origin of particular orders – battalion commander, a Pioneer order or some other.

Given the impossibility of carrying out their original task with the South Africans, the Company Commander took the remainder of his platoons that were working in the front line area to the CO of 10/Argylls and set about improving their strong point at s.17.c.7.7. (ie in the old German front line). From here the men were taken to Green Quarry (s.23a.4.9) and there dug shelter trenches until 8.30 pm. From this place, having reported to Brigade (the advanced HQ of which was in Caterpillar Valley), the men were relieved.

Nos 3 and 4 Platoons were ordered from the rear to Montauban Alley at 5.30 pm and moved up to Longueval at 12.30 am on 19 July to follow up an attack by 19/DLI (Bantam Battalion) and help them prepare a new defence line on their objective. In the event the attack did not take place, and instead, until daylight, they dug 120 yards of trench along the Guillemont road between Delville Wood and Waterlot Farm. The War Diary notes,

This portion was originally allotted to the REs but, owing to their officer being wounded, the section went back to their HQ.
Further orders were issued about work in Longueval, but these were

cancelled, in large measure due to the chaotic conditions of control caused by the German counter-attacks, and at 5.30 pm the Company was ordered back to its bivouac at Carnoy.

B Company

This Company, generally attached to the South African Brigade, had spent its time before 14 July very much as the others – working on roads, light railways, new dugouts in captured positions, such as Bernafay Wood, and making good German defences that could be adapted for British use.

On 14 July at 9 am it was

Detailed to cut CT from Longueval southwards to join road s.17.c.9.7 to s.17.c.4.1. Unable to get on work owing to enemy shelling position and barrage south of same, until 3.30 pm. Completed trench at 11 pm.

On 15 July at 9 am the Company found itself in Delville Wood.

I Platoon carried wire and reported to OC D Company 2/South African Infantry. Found them expecting an attack and lined trenches until 4 pm. No wiring done. Remainder dug support trench behind 2/South African Infantry HQ – 138 yards.

On 16 July at 9 am the Company was detailed to wire the east side of Delville Wood from Princes Street northwards, working in reliefs of two platoons. The first platoon found it impossible to get on with the job, but the second had wired 42 yards by 2.30 am on the 17th, which

Taking up medical stores using a light railway.

was then completed during the night of the 17th. Meanwhile, the Company had moved its HQ forward to a position in Montauban Alley about 150 yards west of the northern tip of Bernafay Wood. On the 17th various platoons worked on a front line trench at s.18.a.5.9: 40 yards were completed by noon, the next platoon dug another 50 yards by 5 pm (and subsequently helped to repulse an enemy attack at 10.30 pm), whilst another 50 yards was added by midnight.

The 19th July was spent in a massive operation to dig a long communication trench, Folly Trench, from the northern tip of the remnants of Trônes Wood to Pall Mall. This started at 1.45 am and included assistance from 64 Field Company RE and D Company of 9/Seaforths. At 11 pm two platoons had to carry wire up to the south west corner of Delville Wood, but no work was done because of the heavy fire and in any case the men had to be evacuated from the wood because of the barrage that was due at 3 am for the next British attack.

C Company

This Company was attached to 27 Brigade and had been engaged in the usual variety of tasks since the assault of 1 July – consolidating Glatz Redoubt, improving road and track communications across the old front line to the new British positions, wiring around Bernafay Wood and digging new communication trenches. On the night of 13 July seven men went out with the Brigade Major to tape out the jump off points for the various battalions in the Brigade. When it came to the actual assault, platoons were split up amongst the attacking infantry and given very specific tasks to accomplish, that is the construction of strong points known as Keeps. Thus 9 Platoon was to construct Keep No 1 at s.17.a.1.2; 10 Platoon Keep No 2 at s.17.a.9.8; 11 Platoon Keep No 3 at s.11.d.6.4; and 12 Platoon Keep No 4 at s.11.c.3.8.

The first and second line of the German trenches having been captured, Captain Armstrong went forward under heavy machine-gun fire to reconnoitre the site for Keep No 1, but found position was commanded from High Wood, and impossible to work in during day time, and so No 9 Platoon under heavy shell fire dug a fire trench at s.22.a.9.5 to 100 yards to the west, having 9 casualties. Nos 10, 11 and 12 Platoons at about 7 am reached Clarges Street, and finding 10/Argylls there, with Germans in close contact in front, proceeded to help to dig them in. No 10 also commenced work on Keep at s.17.b.2.3. During this work active sniping was carried on by the enemy which was replied to by our men, several snipers being seen to fall, whilst

16 prisoners were captured by No 12 Platoon under Second Lieutenant Keating and sent back under escort to Caterpillar Valley. At 4 pm the Company, less No 9 Platoon, returned to Caterpillar Valley and at 8 pm to Oxford Copse. No 9 Platoon remained and dug and wired Keep No 1 and s.17.d.1.2, which was immediately occupied by the infantry.

The Company remained in the support area on the 15th, but on the evening of the 16th moved up to Longueval once more. When they arrived in the village (some two hours after they started) they found themselves under heavy shell fire at the junction of Sloane Street and the Montauban track. The officers went forward to examine the work which they had been instructed to carry out, but found this to be impracticable for No 10 Platoon; however No 11 Platoon was able to work on a trench north of Clarges Street. Due to the British barrage that was to be laid on the village and wood, the men were withdrawn in the early hours of the 17th.

At 3 am on the 18th Nos 11 and 12 Platoons proceeded to Caterpillar Valley and from there No 11 Platoon went, at 6.30 am, to Longueval. Here they were held up at Sloane Street, where they had to lie for an hour because of the heavy shelling. They were joined there

Travelling water-butts. Water supply on the Somme was a big problem for both sides. Development of the infrastructure, including water supply, is one of the undersung achievements of the British Army.

by No 12 Platoon, which had had to come through a heavy barrage en route. No 11 Platoon then went on to make a barricade at the junction of Duke Street and Piccadilly and to dig trenches alongside the road. No 12 Platoon, meanwhile, was suffering quite heavy casualties, and were removed back to Caterpillar Valley, where the remainder collected sand bags to take up to No 11 Platoon. At 8.30 pm Nos 9 and 10 Platoons were instructed to complete the work at Duke Street Keep, but it was discovered that this was no longer in British possession and the fire trenches round and about were so congested that it was impossible to do any further work on them. At 1 am the men returned to Oxford Copse, having suffered 21 casualties, only one of whom was killed though three were wounded and missing. This was effectively the end of the Company's participation in the battle.

The Company also had to supervise the divisional water supply. The main distribution point was at Talus Boisé, which was the terminus of a 6 inch main that came from the pumping station at Suzanne. Second Lieutenant J McNicoll had 41 men under command to carry out his task, which included transporting it in tanks on trolleys from Carnoy to be further distributed to points where it could be taken on to the troops in the front line. These three minor distribution points had to be guarded day and night to prevent waste and pollution; the demand for water ranged from 10,000 to 15,000 gallons per day. Due to damage to three of the storage tanks and hosing by shrapnel (a bombardment that also cost this group of men 12 casualties), use had to be made of the canvas troughs erected by the cavalry. There was five of these, each holding 9,000 gallons, whilst Corps had placed another three in position. These also had to be guarded, and eventually two Military Police from 9/Seaforths and fifteen men of the Cyclists' Corps were provided to carry out this duty. With the improvement in the roads, it was possible to use water carts, which arrived on 16 July. Demands on these increased dramatically after 17 July – from four being filled on that date to 30 on the 18th and 41 on the 19th.

D Company

This Company was used on restoring track – for example on 13 July, after six days work, the Maricourt-Montauban road to Bernafay Wood was made usable for horse drawn traffic. On the 14th this was extended to s.23.c.2.8, the road now being known as Pall Mall. They had started work (137 men) at 6 am and completed it at 5 pm. A railway party managed to open up the railway line to Bernafay Wood on the same day. For the next few days repairs were made to another road.

15 July. 8.30 am Put a road through Montauban from Maricourt to Caterpillar Valley. The original track was completely destroyed by shell fire and the road metal scattered. Numerous trees had to be removed.

16 July. 8.30 am Road making continued. Road from Montauban to Bernafay repaired, previously repaired roads metalled with brick.

17 July. 8.30 am Metalling of road continued till 2.30 pm, when company ordered by CRE [Commander Royal Engineers] *9th Division to stand ready for work that night at Longueval.*

Thus at 5 pm men of the Company moved up to the village.

Party of 20 men under Captain Turcan with CSM Brown moved to Longueval to wire in front of Delville Wood and after dusk they marched up Princes Street to the east end of Delville Wood carrying French Wire. Stopped at the edge of wood by barrage and heavy rifle fire, retired to South African Headquarters in reserve trench about s.18.a.4.8. The party then carried up 11 boxes SAA from dump at s.17.a.9.4 to the reserve trench. Things being now quiet the party wired in front of the South African trenches on the east of the wood using some 32 coils of French Wire. Returned to Talus Boisé at 4.45 am.

Meanwhile a party of 50 men had repaired the old German trench between s.17.d.o.5 to s.17.d.6.8 to provide a sheltered, six feet deep, approach to Delville Wood.

This was the last time that the Company was used in the forward part of the battle zone. On 18 July the company assisted with the trench dug from the north of Trônes Wood mentioned before; and over the next couple of days worked around Montauban before being withdrawn on 20 July to Bronfay Farm.

This account of the work of a Pioneer Battalion during the build up to a battle and the six days or so after the initial assault gives some idea of the range of tasks that could be demanded of it and the sort of conditions under which it had to operate. Supply and logistics are a rather neglected facet of the Great War, and I hope that this small section gives some inkling of the scale of what was required.

Chapter Five

THE DEFENDERS OF LONGUEVAL AND DELVILLE WOOD

The account that follows is extracted from a number of German histories. The narrative is not meant to present a coherent action of decisions taken by the Germans at Longueval and Delville Wood, but rather to give an idea of the problems and difficulties that were encountered at various stages during the six or seven weeks that the battle raged in this sector of the Somme. All too often there is a tendency to see things almost entirely from a British perspective, to view their fighting as uniquely sacrificial, when it is also the case that the Germans, too, felt they were being sacrificed, subject to the same inhuman conditions of artillery and machine-gun fire, of thirst, depravation, fear and carnage. It also gives some insight into the levels of courage that were as apparent in the German army as in their British and South African enemy. Rather sadly the efforts of these brave men from Germany are neglected by almost all of their modern

Two French casualties of 1914 buried by the Germans in Delville Wood.

Street cleaning in Longueval before 1916.

compatriots, with a number of honourable and enthusiastic exceptions, perhaps wishing to forget a disastrous phase in their country's history. One does not have to applaud the motives of the powers-that-be in Germany – but their fighting men do deserve a greater recognition of their fortitude and endurance.

163rd (Scheswig-Holstein) Infantry Regiment

This regiment was recruited from the area of the Danish border; the regimental history was produced in 1926 and was written by Holger Ritter, by that time a Lieutenant Colonel, and who had commanded the III Battalion in the field.

The regiment (effectively the equivalent of a British Brigade) had a battle strength of 65 officers and 2,957 men on 1 July when it moved

German soldiers marching past on the Kaiser's birthday, coming up North Street towards the main square in Longueval.

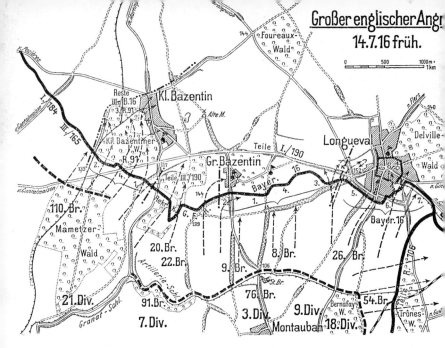

into action, attached to the 185th Division. Although uninvolved in the early fighting, parts of it did become entangled in the fighting around Mametz Wood and Contalmaison. One battalion, the IIIrd, saw action as far away as Puisieux, to the north of Serre, and beyond the extremity of the northernmost part of the battle proper.

On 9 July the regiment was withdrawn to rest and recuperate. It had lost forty officers killed and wounded and just under 900 other ranks. The German system of counting the wounded did not include all those who passed through Aid Posts and the like, for if they could return to the line swiftly they did not necessarily appear in the statistics. However, this is not the place to engage in a discussion about differing

See picture on page 89. This view taken in the summer of 1915 shows Longueval as a sleepy, undisturbed backwater of the western front, a couple of miles behind the front line.

← BAZENTIN RD   FLERS ROAD   DELVILLE WOOD

Longueval in June 1916. Contrast this with the picture on page 40.

methods of body count, though it is one of the more contentious issues of the Great War. Whatever, the regiment had been reduced by a third in a week's fighting.

On 10 July the men used the time to have a good sleep; weapons went into racks and fresh ammunition was distributed. At 10 pm the men went to bed early, but their rest did not last long, because at 12.30 am on 11 July the alarm was raised. Army Group Stein ordered the regiment to Le Sars, six kilometres south west of Bapaume. They were to occupy the German Third Line position on both sides of the road as rear support. At 1.30 am the regimental staff went forward in cars to reconnoitre the position (this gives some idea of how far back from the fighting line this new position was) and the battalions began to move into Le Sars between 4.30 and 5 am. III Battalion occupied the position north of the road, II Battalion in Le Sars itself and to the south.

The extension of the position was begun immediately, tools and dugout materials were available in quantity from a pioneer park in Le Sars. However, it was not long before the regiment was on the move again, for Army Group Stein then ordered it, under cover, to Warlencourt, Ligny-Thilloy and Thilloy where it was to work on extending the Third Position line under the control of the 10th Bavarian Infantry Division, also known as the Burkhardt Division.

Ligny-Thilloy was very busy; staffs and military hospitals were

Today Longueval is once more a peaceful village, freed from the horror of war.

based there and the roads were very crowded, with very heavy traffic day and night, *'so that we could not find any rest that we so desperately needed'*.

On 12 July considerable reinforcements were received from IX Reserve Corps; this consisted of a thousand men, including 56 Unteroffiziers (equivalent to a corporal, but also with the implication of being commission material, hence the under officer title). 9 lieutenants and 7 vizefeldwebels (vice sergeant major) were promoted to Leutnant der Reserve. All of the replacements were distributed to the companies and at the same time it was ordered that all of these men were not to march out with the alarm; instead they were to remain behind with the transport and be given battle training – which they were very much lacking.

The regiment worked at the position until 2.30 pm on 14 July, when the regiment came under the 3d Guard Division, which in turn assigned it to the 6th Guard Infantry Brigade. At 4.45 pm the regimental staff proceeded to Flers, and the regiment was concentrated there by 7 pm.

I/163 occupied the Foureaux Switch Line on a frontage of 1200 metres at the onset of darkness. The trench was a consistent 1.7 metres deep (a shade under six feet) and had good wire obstacles in front. The companies removed one reserve platoon each, who then began to construct new trenches 100 metres behind their company position. The battalion was connected to III/R55 (which means the third battalion of the 55th Reserve Infantry Regiment) on the right and III/163 on the left, which in turn held the position between the Flers-Longueval and Flers-Ginchy roads. That is, it held the ground to the east of Delville Wood. To its left was I/190.

On taking up their positions, both battalions began constructing shelters, which were entirely lacking. They were assisted in this by the small quantity of harassing artillery fire from the British.

II/163 was made available as a reserve to II/26, which was still engaged in heavy fighting in Longueval. The 8th Company was sent into Delville Wood to assist two of the 26th's companies. Its task was to help fill the line which had become broken with parts of the 23rd and 72nd Regiments, which were to the east of the wood (the history refers to it as a forest). However, this was only temporary, and the 8th Company had to bend its left wing back to the north to avoid being outflanked. The 5th Company then came up to cover this flank, moving into the north east of Delville Wood. Other troops were used to try and fill the large gap (700 metres) that existed between those fighting in

Foureaux (ie High) Wood (two battalions of the 26th Regiment) and the 163rd. A company from the Guards Recruit Depot was positioned to extend the line, but came under very heavy fire from German artillery and suffered serious losses as a consequence.

At dawn on 15 July patrols from the 5th Company determined that very strong enemy forces had established themselves in Delville Wood. The British had successfully entrenched themselves at the northern edge of the wood by using the unoccupied eastern edge of it. They positioned four machine-guns there which dominated the Flers-Longueval road. The 9th Company was instructed to clear the northern edge of Delville Wood, but failed in this task because of the strength of

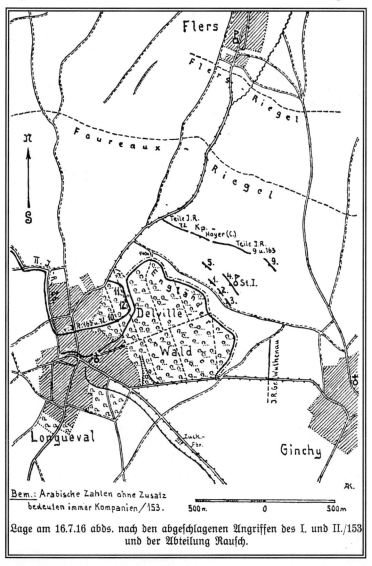

Bem.: Arabische Zahlen ohne Zusatz bedeuten immer Kompanien/153.

500 m. 0 500 m

Lage am 16.7.16 abds. nach den abgeschlagenen Angriffen des I. und II./153 und der Abteilung Rausch.

the South African forces. The Germans also suffered the same problems that had faced the British.

> *Furthermore the forest had such dense undergrowth that penetrating it was vastly difficult. The 9th Company remained lying on the ground until they were reinforced by parts of the 153rd Regiment and with this reinforcement it succeeded, after darkness fell, in rolling up the position of the enemy from the west. Small hand grenade attacks by the enemy during the night were repulsed, but there was such a violent artillery bombardment during the night that there was no thought of extending the position.*

This fire grew even stronger at daybreak, aided in their observation by the enemy planes in large numbers that flew above the positions in Delville Wood. In the afternoon the 11th Company sent out an officer's patrol to find out what was going on and determined that Delville Wood was strongly occupied by the British, who had advanced once more along the eastern edge, but had been restrained by the 153rd. As the evening progressed the 9th Company was forced back some 400 metres, but were reinforced by the 153rd and were able to occupy the north western edge of the wood.

The morning of the 16th was relatively peaceful, and rain in the afternoon was welcome as it kept *'the annoying aircraft away'*. In the course of the day a platoon from the 1st Musketen Battalion, with 7 musketen (automatic rifles) and 31 men was attached to the Ist Battalion. The 5th Company was absorbed into the 6th and 7th because of the level of casualties that had been suffered by all three, and they continued to suffer heavy casualties from the never diminishing artillery fire.

> *At noon on the 16th drum fire was placed upon the right wing of the 8th Company (which was in the area of the orchards near*

View from the German rear area across to Delville and High Woods.

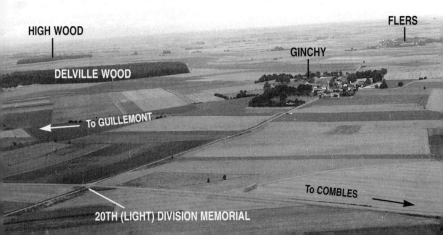

HIGH WOOD

FLERS

DELVILLE WOOD

GINCHY

To GUILLEMONT

To COMBLES

20TH (LIGHT) DIVISION MEMORIAL

Duke Street) and after half an hour the enemy began their attack under the cover of thick smoke and dust. Our men's stand was magnificent. On the right wing they allowed the enemy to come very close in the undergrowth and shot them down immediately in front of the position. At 10.30 pm a heavy bombardment was launched upon both Foureaux and Delville Wood and simultaneously covered the Flers-Longueval road with the heaviest calibre shells. This shelling killed the commander of II/26.

These days were especially severe for the IInd Battalion (ie in and around Longueval itself). The companies had been given tasks that were extremely difficult and that placed monstrous demands on their nerves and physical strength; and that also demanded an exceptional capability, bravery and prudence by their leaders. With almost all of the companies having lost their leaders through wounds or death, yet these companies waited, extremely exhausted and almost never in a position to be able to quench their thirst. In these difficult days their devotion to holding their position could not be surpassed.

Lieutenant Colonel Sick could feel confident in positioning his 163ers wherever they were needed; they never disappointed him. They had endured the most severe situations with a perseverance that was unprecedented. The other regiments were replaced. Infantry Regiment 163 had to endure. Our own 17th Reserve Division was still in front of Arras. The divisions that we were made subordinate to came and went – we remained and were assigned over and over again to the newly arriving ones. With each newly arrived division we must persevere and fight again. We fought with nine different divisions during the Somme, with the 52nd (III/163), 111th, 28th Reserve, 183d, 3d Guard, 185th, 10th Bavarian Reserve, 8th and 5th.

The regiment was, in its different positions, unprotected against the terrible enemy artillery fire of all calibres. It repulsed innumerable enemy attacks. They were always volunteering to execute the most dangerous and daring tasks. The messengers delivering their reports deserve praise above all. The physical and mental demands in the fighting against overpowering numbers of men and resources of material were so monstrous that they are admired today. To highlight the actions of individuals is impossible, as the number of great men was too great. The Musketiers Siedenfrang, Ganz and Radloff voluntarily *reported to carry water from Flers for their absolutely exhausted comrades. Siedenfrang came back with the water, but the other men died a hero's death as a consequence of their devotion to their comrades.*

Although holding the line, the 163rd was not asked to engage in many of the later German counter-attacks that followed until the regiment was finally withdrawn from the sector and the Foureaux Switch Line (known to the British as the Flers Switch) on 23 July. The regiment had suffered just under 500 casualties.

The 153rd Infantry Regiment (8th Thuringian Infantry Regiment, Das Altenburger Regiment).

It was one of the oldest regiments in the German Army Order of Battle, and indeed at mobilisation a minor sensation was caused when the Grand Duke of Sacshsen-Altenburg asked to be allowed to take active command of his regiment, despite the fact that he held the rank of Lieutenant-General. His wish was granted and he went on in due course to command a division.

The regiment had been holding the line for the eight months previous to its arrival on the Somme at Hill 70, near Lens. It was a pleasant time for the men, fields of poppies, well-developed trenches and wire-entanglements, comfortable rest quarters behind the lines and company gardens with fresh produce. The trenches had immaculate dugouts, the trenches were well built and clean and casualties had been very low.

On 14 July orders were received by the 8th Infantry Division to move from Inchy, west of Cambrai to the Bazentin le Petit (Klein Bazentin to the Germans) – Longueval – Flers area. A forced march brought the regiment to the billeting villages of Rocquiny and Le Mesnil, south east of Bapaume at about 9 pm. However, almost immediately the regiment was on the march again, and at 11.30 pm it moved off to a position to the west of Guedecourt

Colonel Zwenger was given the following situation report by Brigade:

The situation is very serious. Longueval, the two Bazentins, also maybe Foureaux Wood are lost to the enemy. Counter-attacks by the 7th Infantry Division are in progress. In the event that they do not succeed, the 16th Infantry Brigade (Regiments 72, 93, 153) is to retake the lost terrain.

The 7th Division attack was a failure, and so the 16th Brigade tried, the 93d on the right, the 72d on the left and the 153d as the Division reserve at the north eastern exit of Guedecourt. This attack also failed. The regiment remained in the vicinity of Guedecourt, in bivouac at its eastern edge. However, during the course of the day III/153 was put under the 26th regiment; and the machine-gun company (Major von Stosch) and II/153 were moved up to the new Brigade reserve, in the hollow north of Flers. That left the regimental commander in control of only one battalion, a few machine-guns and the regimental pioneers. Major von Stosch ignored an order received on 14 July to proceed to the war ministry, on the grounds that changing the leadership of men before an attack should be avoided. Obviously staff jobs were as unpopular with some German regimental officers as they were with their British counterparts.

At this stage on 15 July the situation appeared quiet, the weather was beautiful and the widely dispersed regiment attempted to get some rest after the fatiguing night march. At Guedecourt the only artillery heard was from the German guns, which were on all sides of the village.

At 8.30 pm the regimental commander was ordered to the brigade staff quarters at Le Transloy and received orders that the regiment was to recapture Delville Wood at midnight after artillery preparation. The II and III/153 were to be restored to the regiment, though not all parts of these units were readily available. As far as the regiment was concerned this was all far too rushed, and the commander pleaded for an extension of time in order to organise matters. However this plea was turned down because of the situation elsewhere in the sector, especially to the east of Delville Wood, where matters were worsening by the minute.

Immediately after the conference, which ended at 9.15 pm, the regimental commander issued orders verbally to those at Guedecourt, written to II/153 and sent people out to find III/153 as no-one at regiment or brigade knew where they were!

II battalion was on the right, with its right wing on Point 140, the northern extremity of the wood; with I Battalion on its left, occupying a line some 400 metres long, with the intention of heading through the wood from the north east to the south west. On the left was RIR 107. In fact III/153, under von Stosch, did not get the orders until 10.40 pm, giving them just under an hour and a half to sort themselves out for the attack. The history describes Delville Wood as follows.

Delville Wood was an approximately half kilometre sqaure grove with tall trees and thick undergrowth with severe contours, immediately at the edge of Longueval. It soon changed its look with the constant bombardment from both sides with the tops of the trees growing thinner. However the ground was torn apart and became more confused from day to day, so that orientation in the forest proved to be extraordinarily difficult. The wood was divided by a glade running approximately from the east to the west [ie Princes Street], *described in most messages and reports as 'the great cross glade'. It is further divided by a number of adjacent glades running approximately north to south.*

II/153 battalion commander had to make do with sending orders to his companies and then met the regimental commander at the southern exit of Flers at about 11.20 pm, and voiced his concerns about the timings, also to no avail. His company commanders were briefed as they arrived, the first of which only came through at 11.45 pm. The difficulty of what was taking place, with the lack of reconnaissance, meant that some companies strayed from their line. At last some 300 metres in front of the wood the German line was reached, manned by the remnants of the 9th, 72d and 163d regiments, and was passed over. The attack was delayed here, because no passageways had been cut through the German defensive wire.

Thus it was 12.30 am when the troops first came to a point some 50 metres from the wood and were hit by powerful machine-gun and rifle fire which caused heavy losses and halted the advance, The leading men lay down and returned fire. However, the extreme right of the attack, between Delville Wood and the road (ie west of point 140) made better progress, at least in part because the Germans retained control of the northern part of Longueval. The battalion commander moved over to this area and sent patrols out, which seemed to show that the South Africans had moved further back into Delville Wood, leaving only a machine-gun to hold the Germans up.

Von Stosch decided that he wanted that machine-gun and decided to take it in the rear by outflanking the position, so that this would open the way for the men waiting beyond. At 2 am he penetrated the wood with about 80 men and moved about 200 metres into its interior, but were unable to find the gun in the tangle of undergrowth and the obstacles created by innumerable shell holes. Numbers of men were being killed by machine-gun fire from new sources, and with the increasing light it became imperative to get out of the potential death trap of the wood. At 3.30 am von Stosch got back to his headquarters, accepted the inevitable, and the attackers withdrew, leaving only a small force in the trenches close to Delville Wood.

I/153 had an equally torrid time. They positioned themselves in a hollow, running about 300 metres from the wood's edge; and, like II/153, they had fallen behind the arranged timings. It could only line up for the assault at about 12.30 am and received such a hail of fire as it approached the wood that the attack completely broke down and the men had to scrape protection for themselves close to the edge of the wood. This part of the attack had ground to a bloody halt at 2 am.

The regimental history tries to look on the bright side of things.

The attack of the regiment, in spite of apparent failures, essentially was a great success, because it had blocked any further advance of the Englishmen [sic] out of Delville Wood and, what was still more important, gave flanking support to the Saxon troops fighting further to the left so that they could give renewed resistance. If it did not reach all of the goals, it was a result of the lack of time, which was recognised from all sides. The battalions could only reach their assault positions with half an hour delay. A scheduled preparation of the undertaking through reconnaissance of the enemy, linking up with neighbouring troops, reconnoitering of the terrain, detailed instruction of junior commanders and troops had all been out of the question. The rather pathetic artillery preparation against the forest edge had ceased precisely at midnight, as ordered, therefore a half hour before the attack began; the enemy were alerted and took full advantage of the fact.

The regimental headquarters were based in the southern part of Flers, as were various other parts of the regiment, including III/153. At 10 am the commanding officers of the two regiments, 153d and 26th met to discuss what Rausch, commanding the 26th, considered to be new developments. He was of the opinion that the British troops were surrounded in the north and the south and that the great glade was in German hands except for the eastern exit. He proposed to use the 153d and fresh troops to clear the rest of the glade, whilst first systematically clearing the northern part of Delville Wood. Rausch was known as very dependable, very prudent and outstandingly brave leader, and the various formation commands had no problem in confirming his plan. He was given four companies from 153, but in the event did not use one of them, the pioneers, and these were sent back to Gueudecourt.

See map page 93

The attack was a complete failure, and Rausch himself was killed at 10 pm. In fact the report of von Stosch had been the more accurate, as was shown by a patrol in the evening of 17 July, and all that Rausch's troops had done previously was to mistake one of the adjacent glades for the great glade (Prince's Street). Absolutely nothing of any

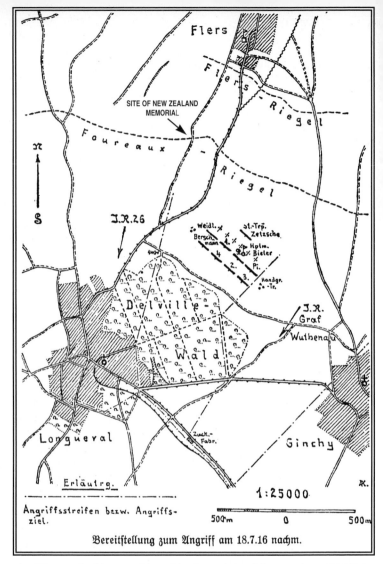

Bereitftellung zum Angriff am 18.7.16 nachm.

significance had been achieved in the attack of the evening of 16 July.

The situation on the German side was quite chaotic, with control of the units in the sector extremely difficult.

Once anybody has been in the situation, it is possible to understand how such a disorderly situation could be possible. Commanders had to deal with troops from a whole range of units. The reliability of junior leaders, especially as regards knowledge, tactical understanding and the quality of their reporting was made highly questionable by the heavy shelling and the destruction of Delville Wood.

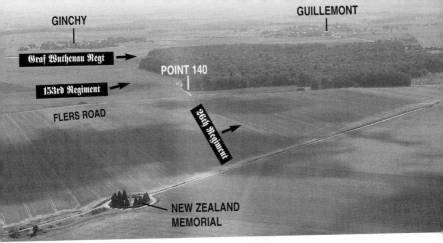

GINCHY | GUILLEMONT |

Graf Wuthenau Regt →

153rd Regiment →

POINT 140

FLERS ROAD

26th Regiment →

NEW ZEALAND MEMORIAL

Contrast aerial photograph with map on page 100.

This situation continued through the 17th, when another attack that evening similarly failed.

Until now the counter-attacks against Delville Wood were counter thrusts, or were an inadequate combination of counter thrust and counter-attack. The were quite sufficient to prevent any further advance by the enemy, but they brought us no further forward. Therefore it became necessary for a more proper counter-attack, which was ordered for 18 July.

The attack commenced with a systematic shelling. Some unified command had been established in Longueval, and so a complete withdrawal of all troops was executed during the night of the 17th, positions being taken to the north, about 200 metres away from the village. In addition, a number of heavy mortar batteries had been brought up from Verdun to provide heavy fire on the British trenches, whilst the artillery set about counter-battery work, trying to find and destroy the British guns. In parenthesis it is worth noting that one consequence of the Somme was the abandonment on 11 July by the Germans of their offensive at Verdun – but the downside of this was the availability of specialist weapons, such as the trench mortars, for the Somme front.

The Germans aimed to capture the old German front line – that is from the southern edge of Longueval to the Guillemont sugar refinery. This latter position was also to be attacked by a number of troops armed with small flame-throwers. The artillery bombardment on the British lines began at 12.45 and the assault itself was scheduled for 4.45 pm. In addition, a Storm Troop section of IV Army was attached to the attack.

The attack went according to plan, and penetration of the wood was achieved, though there was heavy hand to hand fighting and there were considerable problems from enemy soldiers who had been passed over in the advance. There was a problem establishing contact with German troops on the left and that the eastern corner of the wood was still in British hands. The situation was received in a simple report.

> *Southern edge of forest reached, no more officers, the men are exhausted.*

The history goes on to comment on the importance of two particular groups in the army – an importance that had emerged over the two years of bitter conflict. One of them was the young, 'tactically undertrained' company commanders. The other was battalion commanders.

> *Generally they were drawn into this war as Lieutenants, and had previously in peace occasionally led a company in a battalion. It took ten years of military experience and tactical determination in order to shape a company leader. Thus it was good luck if a battalion had great commanders.*

What is being said is something that Ludendorff was to note in his writings – that Verdun and the Somme were to 'kill off' much of the pre-war German army, and its reservoir of trained talent, a legacy of the thorough military peacetime establishment that had been evolved in Imperial Germany. This had been the fate of the British Army much earlier in the war, with a significant part of the Regular Army gone by the end of 1914.

The author of the history chooses this moment to dwell on another aspect of battle – the problem of water.

> *It was a very interesting test of one's own life to see how long one could endure without washing oneself, let alone shave. The small quantities of water that were brought forward from the rear, by dint of great labour, was for use in the front line only. (The Englishman had solved the difficulty of supplying drinking water by constructing more than 192 kilometres of water pipes and over one hundred pumping stations during the preparation for the attack.) So five days passed without a drop of water on the hands and face of the writer of these lines, and to his shame that he felt completely well nevertheless. However this was entirely due to the exceptionally favourable weather; it was almost constantly beautiful, sunny weather, very warm during the day; however, it was also warm during the night so that troops could endure in the open without many losses due to sickness.*

At 6pm a complication came about with command to the rear, for a British shell knocked out regimental headquarters. A German officer wrote home about this experience.

Two direct hits went into the staff quarters, a house at the southern exit of Flers. The first shell only brushed through the roof of the next building; however the second struck it. The quarters were in ruins; my lad, Elle, and two telephone orderlies were severely wounded by the shell that entirely destroyed our cellar.

While the shells howled I was writing orders dictated by the commander. In a fraction of a second the lighted tallow on the bottle went out; mortar and stones rained down upon us. We and

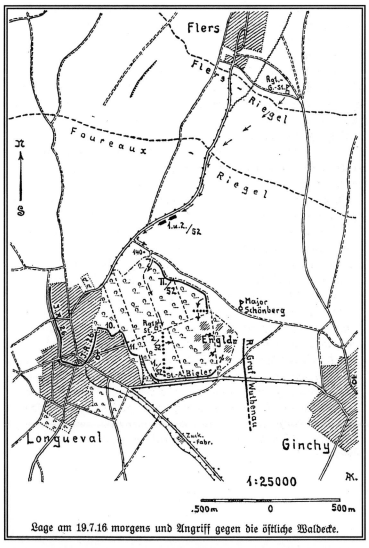

Lage am 19.7.16 morgens und Angriff gegen die östliche Waldecke.

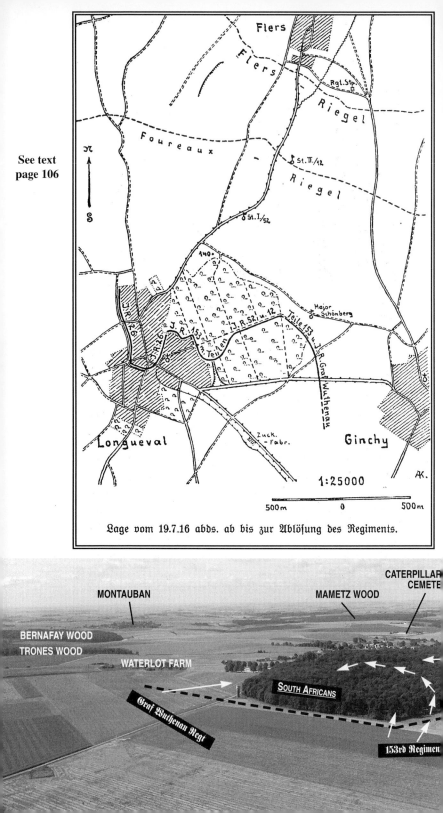

See text
page 106

1:25000

500m   0   500m

Lage vom 19.7.16 abds. ab bis zur Ablösung des Regiments.

MONTAUBAN

MAMETZ WOOD

CATERPILLAR
CEMETE

BERNAFAY WOOD
TRONES WOOD

WATERLOT FARM

SOUTH AFRICANS

Graf Wuthenau Regt

153rd Regimen

the chairs flew to one side. The Colonel's torch was turned on and the light cone moved along the ground until it was there in front of me. 'Would you please pick up my monocle that lies in front of your feet?' In complete silence the Colonel placed the broken pieces of his eye piece with a letter that had previously lain before him on the table, and turned towards the buried cellar entrance. With the words, 'Into the pitfall with you, my dear B(öhme)', he pushed me in front of himself up the stairs into daylight, whilst behind us the crashing beams of the roof crash through into the cellar.

The headquarters were moved to the sunken road to the south east of Flers, on the road to Ginchy.

Bitter fighting continued in the wood, and the British continued to probe from the east, finding gaps in the German line.

A more powerful English forward thrust advanced through the gaps that were still not closed, especially through the quite concealed sunken road, lying just east of the village, and caused the mostly leaderless 153d great distress. Well directed flanking fire caused numerous casualties, and especially effective were South African snipers concealed in the trees. So the fighting against the enemy in the forest gradually went back and forth, connections were lost, the confusion became even greater, until finally darkness made an overview of the situation quite impossible.

It would be impossible for the Germans to move out of Delville Wood with the situation on the left so unsatisfactory and this is how things stood at 6 pm on 18 July. The consequence of this was that the Germans began to fall back, with only the right wing holding on to the southern edge of the wood. Wounded officers made their way back to III/153 headquarters, and Major Schönberg decided (at 6.50 pm) on his own authority to take up the IIId and the available parts of the IId via the road to Ginchy. Their aim was to clear the wood of the remaining British and establish a clear connection with German troops on the left.

The officer mentioned above also sent a description home of the commander of III/153, Major Schönberg.

It was a touching sight: this white bearded man amidst his shot up battalion! The old gentleman had crouched for the greater part of a day in a trench that was hardly knee deep and his battalion had torn forward over and over again up to the north east edge of Delville Wood. How close this leader and his men came in the hardship and danger they underwent nobody

Major Schönberg.

can portray. The order that he gave to the III Battalion at the commencement of the fighting will always live in the history of III/153. 'We no longer have a flag here, my children, however, where my white beard flows, so stands the IIId Battalion'. So thus it was during those difficult days... It deeply affected me when I brought the news to our Papa Schönberg that the regiment had been mentioned in the army report. The old man turned round and cried about his, 'children, who fought here and had bled and had been killed'.

As the evening progressed, matters were still unclear. Early on 19 July the regimental adjutant (equivalent to a British Brigade Major) went up to see what was going on on the left flank. He found Schönberg in his battle headquarters, who managed to convince him of the British presence in the eastern part of the wood.

He then came across two company commanders of the 52d who had been ordered to clear the eastern edge of the wood; they held maps in their hands that meant nothing to them, so disorienting had things become. Since it seemed that their assault was doomed to failure, the regimental commander took them in hand. Running the risk of keeping them close together, he took them almost to the village and then took a half left turn into the wood, emerging at the great glade. This quite drastic action was taken to try and clear the wood. The group of 200 men were formed along Princes Street and placed approximately one and a half paces apart. They would then enter the wood to the south of the ride and pivot leftwards, creating a three hundred metre arc that was making its way steadily eastwards, 'towards the sun'. This final piece of pressure, looking like a well regulated exercise, had the desired effect, and a mass of prisoners (190 men and three machine-guns) were collected on the south eastern edge of Delville Wood.

The prisoners there were South African, part of English, part of Dutch descent: all were magnificent looking men. Some of them carried our men on makeshift stretchers, men who had all been wounded in the great advance yesterday – they were Storm

106

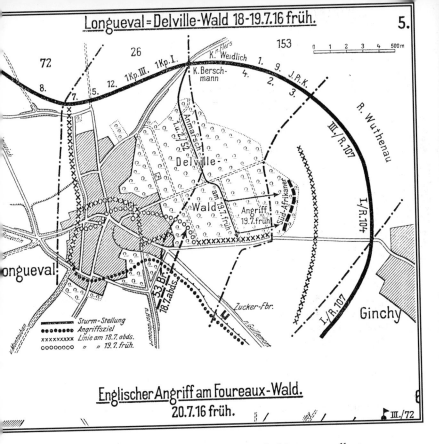

Englischer Angriff am Foureaux-Wald.
20.7.16 früh.

Troopers. The Englishmen treated our wounded in an excellent manner while in their short captivity. Their medical welfare, food, drink, smoking materials were all amply offered in a friendly manner. Amongst them were things that were truly unobtainable delicacies to the poor Germans: mineral water, champagne, gin, chocolates, hams, biscuits etc., etc. It confirmed once again that in general the Englishman was a decent adversary, and that against them, if the expression may be allowed, it was a pleasure to conduct war. It was very different from their allies, the French, who acted with a distinct spite at every opportunity and who were responded to with honesty by our side!

Then the regimental history goes on, somewhat wearily,

So finally the entire Delville Wood was in our hands – or maybe for two or three hours duration, until almost all was lost again.

What happened had an inevitability about it that soldiers on both sides

107

were beginning to realise.

When the Englishmen discovered that there were no more of their troops in the wood, they immediately opened an exceptionally powerful artillery shelling on the southern edge. This was then followed by strong infantry attacks which pressed our line back far into the northern edge of the forest. To be sure Major Schönberg, assisted by two companies of the 52d, undertook a new advance and who initially made good progress. This was brought to a stop by the most severe enemy artillery and mortar fire. At about midday our line lay close to the south of the great crosswise glade; only on the right wing did weak forces get further forward, but they were without contact with the main line.

The condition of the troops ridiculed any description after four days of endless fighting; everyone was at the end of their strength and men from different regiments were all mixed together – 153, 72, 26, 163, 9, 52. None of the commanders, such as were either still alive or capable of fighting, knew his men, and few men knew their leader. Control in the completely chaotic wood had ceased completely, so that for many men there was the overwhelming temptation to look for a connection to their regiment in the rear – and this led to a slipping away of men in the front line, wherever that might be. Actually such a clearing process had more advantages than disadvantages, because whoever still endured with his leader in the front out of conviction was certainly someone who could be relied upon.

The belief was now general that the conquered ground could only be held by fresh troops.

On the evening of 19 July II/12 was ordered to roll up the western part of Delville Wood up to the southern edge and join there with 153d and 52d, who would then turn their attention to the eastern edge. But this attack bogged down at the great crosswise glade and had hardly gained anything. Everyone dug in where they were, approximately in the middle of the forest, with the Englishmen close by them

Now came the tactical enlightenment – delivered from the practical experience of the fighting men, the enlightenment that the inferior and average man was the quickest to recognise. This was the only system of fighting by which weaker troops with weaker artillery and number of planes could successfully persevere and hold out for a long time. If we had the entire forest *or if the Englishmen had it, it was only small thing for the artillery to make any stay in the wood impossible in a very short time; maybe the property would change hands again in an infantry attack, and then a new game would start.*

And this description of the tactics to be followed was not far from the truth. If both sides had men in Delville Wood, then the artillery was constrained and a sort of modus vivendi emerged; once one side or the other was ejected, then the full force of their artillery could be brought to bear. This was the reality of the situation in Delville Wood for the next several weeks. The British retained their control of Longueval and the relatively secure access from Montauban. Their right flank was secured by possession of the sugar factory and their left by the high ground near the windmill. The German hold was secured by their tenure of the northern extremity of Longueval, covered by Wood Lane and High Wood on their right, whilst the left was guarded by Ginchy and Guillemont. The folds in the ground provided a reasonable covered approach from Flers. Until events moved on either flank, it was difficult to see how tenure of Delville Wood could be made permanent by either side.

There is, of course, much more that can be written about the German efforts at Delville Wood; but these accounts bring home the

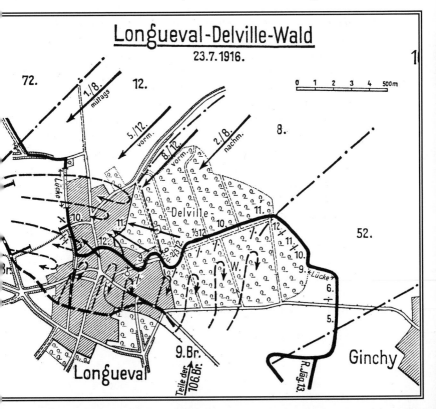

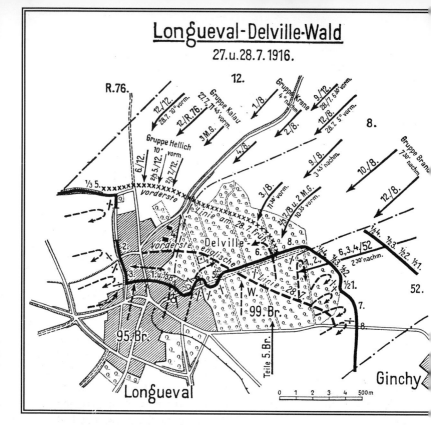

Longueval-Delville-Wald
27.u.28.7.1916.

nature of the fighting that the Germans endured; and when examined it will be found that there was not that much difference in the experience of both sides. The 153d Regiment left Delville Wood finally on the 22nd, to go out to rest at Le Transloy, but were called back within twelve hours to man part of the Switch Line by High Wood for a couple of days, suffering relatively few casualties. On 28 July it was relieved once more, and finally set off to the rear areas to rest and recuperate, taking over billets in the region of Le Cateau, to the east of Cambrai. Its ten days on the Somme had cost it just under fourteen hundred casualties – some fifty percent of its strength.

Germans back in Longueval after the spring offensive, 1918.

Chapter Six

THE LONG HAUL: INCIDENTS IN THE CAPTURE OF DELVILLE WOOD - THE BRITISH VIEW

The experiences of the King's Royal Rifle Corps and the 17th (Northern) Division.

1/KRRC – late July 1916.

Towards the end of July the 2nd Division came in to take over the Delville Wood sector from the 3rd Division, with the 5th Division responsible for the bulk of Longueval itself. The following account is taken from the war record of 1/KRRC, a member of which was to win the Victoria Cross during the course of the fighting.

The 2nd Division had been serving in the Vimy Ridge area for some time, and this was its first time on the Somme. There was a long approach march for part of the way; from Longeau (where the men were detrained), just east of Amiens, to Morlancourt, a distance of sixteen miles. This was done in about five and a half hours marching time (11.45 pm – 7 am with about two hours for stops, not bad considering the period of time the men had spent in the trenches and that much of the march was in the dark). It is also important to remember that the roads were certainly not of the quality that they are now; by and large they were often little more than tracks, rutted, sometimes cobbled, which made things slippery, especially with ammunition boots, and with a definite concave shape.

The confused situation in Delville Wood was evidenced by the variety of orders that the Battalion received. On 24 July it moved up to the sand pits at Meaulte, having been briefed on the position it was to occupy and the attack in which it was to be engaged. At 1.30 pm information came through that the Battalion was to occupy the firing line that night. Just before the Battalion was due to move off, at 5.50 pm, news came through that the relief had been altered and that the Battalion was to take over all of the trenches in Delville Wood instead of the line by Waterlot Farm, as originally specified. Whilst the Battalion was moving up towards Carnoy the orders were changed again, with the Battalion taking over the northern part of Delville Wood that night, the southern part the following night.

See map page 109

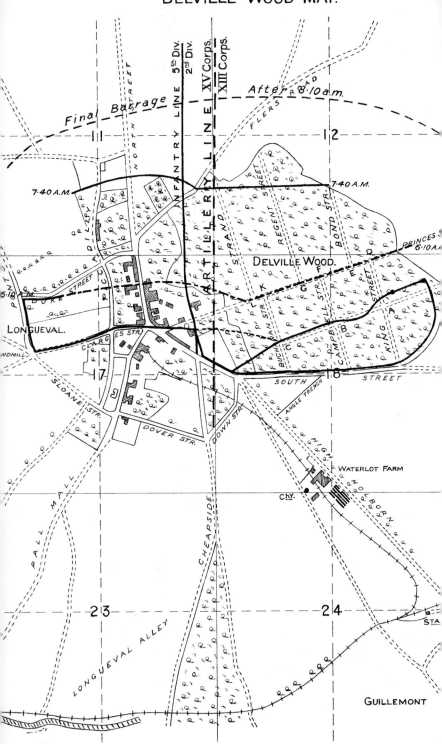

DELVILLE WOOD MAP.

XIII

Map. Y.I.

Scale 1:10,000

WARREN & SON LTD LITH

The road from Bernafay Wood to Longueval, where our Headquarters were to be, was extremely 'unhealthy' and just about as unpleasant a walk as one could find anywhere. The Germans, of course, knew all this country to an inch, and realised that we must use it, consequently they strafed it continuously. We had a few casualties going up, which was lucky when compared with the regiment we were relieving, which had fifty. The worst part of this lane was about a mile long, and the whole of this portion of the road and each side of it had been ploughed up by shell fire. The relief took a long time to complete, as none of our officers had seen a yard of the line before they went in with their men.

The Battalion created a new company by removing a platoon from three of the existing companies, and kept one company in support in Montauban Alley.

Our Headquarters had a very good dugout, but was overcrowded by orderlies, signallers etc., and situated in the worst part of the village from a point of view of the enemy's shells. This is accounted for by the fact that the Germans made this good dugout, and consequently knew exactly where it was situated.

With the coming of daylight on 25 July it was possible for the CO to go around the line.

There were dead lying all over the ground in and out of the wood. Our portion of the line, and that to the left and right of us, was extremely complicated: the part that the Battalion held faced north, east, south and west! Our own guns did as much damage as those of the enemy, and we were not in touch with any of the batteries either by telephone or by visual signalling.

Five Germans surrendered to us during the morning, and several more either wanted to or, until shot, were going to try one of their foul tricks. In the evening we took over part of the Gordons' line in Delville Wood.

All was relatively quiet on 26 July – a German bombing attack in the early hours, more casualties caused by British 'drop shorts' whilst six eleven man patrols investigated the German positions. The attack was to be launched at 6 am on 27 July, with 23/R Fusiliers on the left.

At 6 am B and D Companies, advancing under our barrage, captured Princes Street with little loss, and proceeded to consolidate it. We found the trench full of dead and wounded Germans, and amongst the debris were two damaged machine-

guns. *Meanwhile C and A Companies had moved up in support, and a company of the Royal Berkshire Regiment had formed a defensive flank on the right. A and A Companies moved through B and D and, protected by a barrage, occupied the red line (marked 6.10 am on the accompanying map) and likewise consolidated it.*

See map page 110

Our heavies [ie heavy artillery] *at this period were shooting short, so urgent messages were sent to the Artillery liaison officer to have this remedied. At 9 am Captain Stafford reported that the losses in B Company were heavy and that the Germans were evidently preparing a counter-attack. An hour later this developed into a heavy bomb attack, and an urgent appeal for more bombs was promptly met.*

The CO, Lieutenant Colonel Denison DSO describes the fight.

Owing to the Company forming the defensive flank not having thrown its right flank out far enough to the edge of the wood and connecting with B Company, the Germans were able to creep in behind Princes Street line. They gained seventy yards but were driven back forty yards, chiefly owing to the gallantry of Sergeant Woodward. This bomb attack decimated B Company, and D Company suffered heavily also. Captain Howell was wounded about 9 am, but continued to carry on his duties, acting with great gallantry. It was greatly due to his efforts that the Germans counter-attack was driven off with tremendous loss.

At the same time C and A Companies were heavily attacked from the north and the north east. Fighting took place at fifteen yards range with bombs and rifle fire. The Germans suffered very heavily.

I tried to send up SOS rockets, but only two went off properly, the rest had got damp. Fighting went on incessantly, chiefly sniping from shell holes, the Germans trying all the time to creep in on my flank between the various lines.

B and D Companies were heavily attacked from their right flank. More bombs arrived, and some bombers behaved with great gallantry and drove back the Germans. The German method of bomb attack was to bomb up the new trench with snipers on each flank.

The enemy put a very heavy barrage on old British front line – South Street, the Dressing station, Longueval Village and Longueval Alley – traversing the road between Angle trench and South Street with a machine-gun from the direction of trenches north of Waterlot Farm. This barrage was kept up till dark, making reinforcing very difficult.

22/Royal Fusiliers now arrived, some were used as carrying parties for bombs and ammunition. The remainder I ordered to assist in defending my right flank on the east face, with their right on the left bomb post towards Princes Street. Owing to the difficulty of providing guides for various parties, the 22nd did not take up the position I intended them to.

About 5.15 pm two companies 17/R Fusiliers and 17/Middx arrived having suffered heavily coming up.

At 6 pm it was reported to me that my centre post on the south east flank had been knocked out by shell fire. The Germans attacked and were driven back.

Two platoons 17/R Fusiliers reinforced posts with two Lewis guns. I then sent one company 17/R Fusiliers to reinforce, and eventually relieved my C Company. I then arranged where the companies of 17/Middx should go to relieve my companies and, if necessary, to try and reinforce them by night. This was difficult owing to the heavy sniping going on, and also to the fact that they would be very exposed to view.

A report came to me just before dark, time unknown, that both my left and centre posts had been captured, and that the Germans were massing to attack, the officer in left post having been killed; this I reported to Lieutenant Colonel Fenwick (17/R Fusiliers), as it made my position very insecure, and if information was correct, extremely critical. I eventually decided to use the company of 22/R Fusiliers to form a defensive flank behind the two posts and to dig themselves in. As I was waiting for the general to come up at 11 pm, I was unable to go round until about two hours afterwards. Captain Gell, 22/Fusiliers, informed me that it was a false alarm, and that the posts were all intact and strongly held, and he had not formed the defensive flank.

In the early morning I withdrew the Battalion to Montauban Alley.

During the course of this battle another VC was won in Delville Wood, this one by Sergeant Albert Gill of 1/KRRC, a thirty six year old man who came from Birmingham. He was gazetted for the VC on 26 October 1916.

The enemy made a very strong counter-attack on the right flank of the battalion, and rushed the bombing post, after killing

Sergeant A Gill winning his VC in Delville Wood; he is buried in Delville Wood Military Cemetery.

all the company bombers. Sergeant Gill rallied the remainder of his platoon, none of whom were skilled bombers, and reorganised his defences, a most difficult and dangerous task, the trench being very shallow and much damaged. Soon afterwards the Germans nearly surrounded his men by creeping up through the thick undergrowth, and commenced sniping at about twenty yards range. Although it was almost certain death, Sergeant Gill stood boldly up in order to direct the fire of his men. He was killed almost at once, but not before he had shown his men were the enemy were, and thus enabled them to hold up their advance. By his supreme devotion to duty and self-sacrifice he saved a very dangerous situation.

Gill's body was one of the relatively few recovered and identified from the wood, and he is now buried in Delville Wood Military Cemetery,

IV.C.3. He was a member of the forward line of companies, trying to hold the forward (northern) edge of the wood.

One of the battalions that had supported the attack was 17/R Fusiliers. They have a well-written Battalion history, which gives some graphic descriptions of the battle in Delville Wood.

The 27th was ghastly in the extreme. 17/R Fusiliers were not one of the attacking battalions, but it is an open question whether they would have suffered more than they did in Longueval Alley. For when 99 Brigade attacked the wood the enemy's guns opened fire on the whole area and on Longueval Alley especially, or so it seemed. All communications with the wood were very quickly broken as high explosive and shrapnel lashed the trenches in which the Fusiliers crouched, trying to take cover from that awful storm.

At 2 pm A and B Companies of the 17th were placed at the disposal of 99 Brigade and moved up to Delville Wood. Major Mackenzie, guided by one of the Battalion scouts who on the previous night had wandered into Delville Wood by mistake, led the two companies to the KRRC Headquarters just inside the southern edge of the wood. On the way up the shell fire was terrific and B Company lost several men, though Angle Trench was a fairly safe approach to the wood.

On arrival at the Headquarters of the Rifles two platoons with two Lewis guns were sent to reinforce the posts, while one of the companies relieved C Company of the KRRC. The front line at this period was a chain of shell holes and blown-in trenches just inside the far edge of the wood.

The horrors of that place were now everywhere evident. The fearful havoc created by our barrage of the early morning, when no less than 369 guns of all calibres had poured a continuous storm of shells upon the unfortunate enemy, had piled destruction upon destruction. Branches of trees had been thrown about in all directions; the thick undergrowth of the wood was pitted with shell holes into which the enemy had crept for shelter – the whole place was in a state of indescribable confusion – to the attackers it was almost like creeping through a jungle, not knowing where the enemy was lurking or at what minute he might be encountered. The dead were everywhere – equipment littered the ground; and, above all, in the momentary pauses between one shell-burst and another, the moans or agonised cries of the wounded, calling for water or assistance, lent a final

117

With scenes such as this common place during the war, it is hardly surprising that many veterans were unwilling to discuss their experiences.

touch to an altogether ghastly scene.

The Battalion had landed in France at the end of November 1915, and this was the first occasion when their casualties amongst other ranks alone had exceeded a hundred.

An anonymous account tells something of what took place to A and C Companies during their time in the wood from the early hours of the 28th.

At dawn on the 28th the stretcher-bearers were guided to the worst cases which were quickly evacuated. Major Mackenzie kept his runners busy in maintaining touch with the advanced posts. The shelling was fairly bad, but the chief trouble was water. The heat was terrific and the fumes made matters worse. But in the afternoon RSM Haines, by dint of a good bit of work, got some water (of which there was a plentiful supply in Longueval Alley) up to Major Mackenzie who sent word to the firing line asking for water carriers. The water was brought up by the train section. That evening the 17 Middlesex reinforced the depleted forces and further ammunition arrived; the counter-attack launched by the enemy was cheerfully and successfully dealt with. A timely artillery barrage cut off a large body of Germans who were practically wiped out by bombs and rifle and machine-gun fire. During the succeeding lull the 9th Essex relieved the 17th Royal Fusiliers, the last of whom left the dreadful wood at 11 am on the 29th.

118

This attack had captured more or less the whole of Delville Wood, while on the left the 5th Division had gained the better part of Longueval, leaving only the orchards and posts north of the village in the hands of the enemy. However, the position was far from securely held.

The 17th (Northern) Division

This division had already taken part in the battle of the Some, from its earliest days until it was relived on 11 July, in the area around Contalmaison and Mametz Wood. It had suffered just under five thousand casualties.

On 1 August 1916, 52 Brigade moved up to a bivouac near the ruins of Fricourt and prepared to move up the line and take over that part held by the 5th Division in Longueval and Delville Wood. The move up took place once twilight set in, and involved a lengthy march in the dark.

The battle line that night was a marvellous spectacle. Flashes of guns, rockets, flares and the variegated colours of the Very lights lit up the whole horizon, and for all the world looked like a gigantic firework display. Now and then an extra glare would indicate something explosive having been hit by a shell, and the village of Longueval was burning brightly from the incendiary shells that had been poured into it.

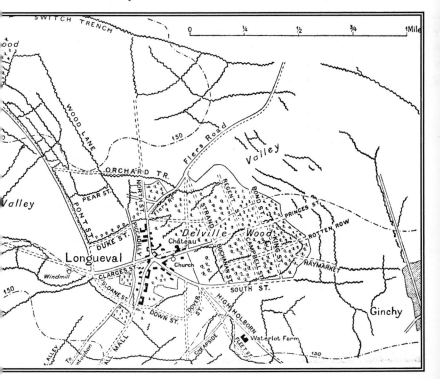

The situation in this area had become so complicated on the ground that the relief took a long time, not completed until dawn.

For a fortnight there had been confused fighting along the north margin of the wood and in the orchards at the north end of the long village. The day before the relief an attack on the enemy position at the latter end of the sector had failed. Day and night for more than a fortnight the village and wood had been persistently shelled by the enemy with guns of various calibres, from field pieces to 5.9 howitzers, throwing big crumps. The fire came from three directions – In front from the rising ground of the Bapaume ridge west of Flers; on the left from the ground north of High Wood still partly held by the enemy, and from the right about Ginchy. The village and Delville Wood were, for the enemy, on the skyline, for they stood on the crest of the Combles-Thiepval ridge, the outlying high ground running roughly parallel to the Bapaume ridge. From both ridges long spurs ran out and overlapped, giving on our left well-covered positions for batteries using indirect fire. The result of this prolonged bombardment was that all the ground was badly cratered, trenches had been reduced to strings of shell holes, and it was very difficult to identify the positions marked on our trench maps. In the information provided for the relief, posts were named as occupied which did not exist. To add to the difficulties of the sector our aircraft did not so completely dominate the situation as had been the case on 1 July, and the German planes were active and enterprising. The enemy was extending a new trench system in the immediate front and held positions close up to our ill-defined line, and from these kept up a deadly fire of snipers and machine-guns, so that in front any movement by daylight was difficult.

The Divisional War Diary notes the situation as reported by 5th Division.

Our line extends along Pont Street to Duke Street, thence across to Piccadilly into Delville Wood, with posts believed to be at these points:

> *a: Junction of trenches in Pear Street at s.11.c.2.5*
> *b: Junction of Pear Street and Wood Lane*
> *c: s.11.d.0.5*
> *d: s.11.d.3.6 (in North Street)*
> *e: Corner of orchard at s.11.d.5.7*

The diary goes on to note,

There appeared however to be considerable doubts as to the position of these posts, more especially as the existence of Orchard Trench, and the fact of its being held by the enemy, had only just become known. The fact that Orchard Trench had been dug and occupied by the enemy was believed to have been the chief cause of the failure of the 5th Division's attack on the night of 30/31 July.

That night post a and b were identified and relieved, but the rest could not be found at the time; in the meantime there was no contact with the brigade on the right in the wood. The only deep dugout was near the ruins of the church (to the east of its present location).

When day dawned on 2 August an attempt was made to clear the situation. On the right, in the wood, a defensive flank was formed to the right rear of the line to guard the gap, and patrols went out to gain touch with the 13th [sic – the 13th Division served the whole war in the Middle East, Near East or Gallipoli; meant to be 2nd] *Division in the wood. Other patrols sent to the front of the wood discovered, in its north west corner near the Flers road, two machine-gun detachments of the 5th Division, which had been isolated there for three days, under frequent shell fire, and the men were now without food or water and in a very exhausted condition. They were relieved by a machine-gun*

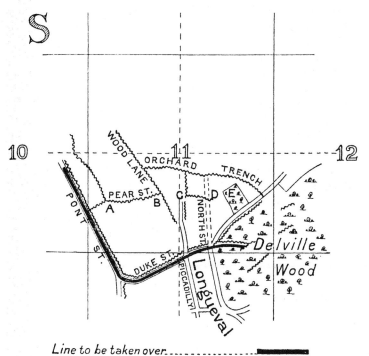

Line to be taken over. . . . . ▬▬▬▬

A, B, C, D, E ; *Posts reported as held in front of line*

Relief of 5th Division by 52nd Brigade at Longueval.

detachment of 52 Brigade. It seemed not unlikely that this represented post e, supposed to be in the orchard on the other side of the Flers road. Further to the left, close to the line, an abandoned British machine-gun and another that had been smashed up by a shell burst were found. The enemy were not only in Orchard trench, but also in the orchards at the north end of the village, and their extreme front seemed to run through the supposed positions reported at c, d and e, their real positions, while they existed, being close in to our front line. It is easy to say that such mistakes should not be made, but in warfare like that of the Somme battlefields there were times and conditions that made it no wonder that they occurred, the only marvel being that they did not occur more often. Positions where every marked feature by which a map can be set has been beaten flat and the outlook is amongst shattered woods and orchards and over ground churned by weeks of shell fire into a stretch of craters, with trench lines hardly distinguishable from the chaos around them – this forms a very different prospect from the trim legibility of neatly squared maps full of clearly shown detail, some of which had ceased to exist in reality.

There was a further problem that the historian of the Division noted. In the 17th, as in all the divisions that had already been heavily engaged at an earlier date in the great battle, there were now many young officers and NCOs who were having their first experience of trench warfare under these difficult conditions. So far they had only seen the practice trenches of the training grounds, and it is more than doubtful if these dummy defences were ever designed to represent a trench position that had all but disappeared in a wild confusion of shell craters and heaps of debris.

It was decided that 52 Brigade should eject the Germans from the position in Orchard Trench and that this would be done during the night hours, after midnight on 4 August. The biggest problem about this lay in the preparatory artillery bombardment; for the British and German lines were close, the British positions ill-defined and it was impossible to evacuate them during daylight hours. As soon as the artillery started up, there was a fierce German response. It struck at the British batteries tucked away to the rear of Caterpillar Wood, at random in the area behind the line and along the communication trenches. On the front line the Germans also used phosphorous gas shells. Men in the front line from the Northumberland Fusiliers and the Duke of Wellington's suffered considerable casualties, many of them from gas.

All were exhausted from the strain of hanging on to trenches in inadequate cover, and so 12/Manchesters were sent up, suffering many casualties in the inadequately constructed communication trenches on their way up.

The attack was launched at 12.40 am, and failed.

After the attack of the night before many of our wounded were lying in the cratered ground of No Man's Land. Some of these close up to the enemy's wire were taken into the German line. Others were rescued by our patrols during the night of 4 August. Captain Benton of the Manchesters was not thus rescued until he had lain for thirty hours in a shell hole without food, water or first-aid. He had been in the Headquarters of his battalion at the outset of the attack, and after the first check he had gone out to obtain information as to the position and help in reorganising the men for a second attempt. He was badly wounded, one of his legs shattered by machine-gun fire. It was a marvel that he survived these hours of lonely agony in No Man's Land.

There is a footnote to this passage.

It was one of the horrors of this prolonged trench warfare that the firing was practically continuous, and it was rarely that there was even a local informal truce to clear the battle-ground after a hard fight. The dead lay unburied in No Man's Land or tangled in the wire; the wounded were often left without help. Sometimes, but very rarely, a brief unofficial truce was arranged by the local commanders at the fighting front, and British and Germans worked together at succouring the wounded and getting them back into their own lines. But this was an irregular proceeding, and higher authority on both armies had a dread of anything like 'fraternisation'.

On 5 August 51 Brigade took over Delville Wood. Officially it was deemed to be within the British lines.

This however was optimism not entirely justified by fact. Only the western margin of the wood and its central southern part were entirely clear of the enemy. There was not even any continuous trench front in existence traversing it from west to east. The line was at best a series of detached fragments of old German trenches, with between them strings of shell craters, improvised into posts. It was a mass of broken tree trunks and fallen branches, often blocking the rides that had once been open roadways through it, with shell holes everywhere, and a tangle of undergrowth, bristling here and there with rusty barbed wire.

The enemy had freely used phosphor gas bombs in the three weeks bombardment, and the poison gas hung in hollows, and drifted among the undergrowth. But there was an even more noisome foulness in the air. Day after day, from soon after sunrise, the heat had been of tropical intensity, and the nights were close and sultry. From end to end Delville Wood was littered, and, in many places heaped, with dead. They had fallen in the days of hand-to-hand fighting when the wood was first penetrated, and under the persistent bombardment that followed. Many of them wore the German field-grey uniform, many the British khaki, and of the latter, numbers bore the badges of the South African Brigade and of Scottish battalions. One of the

Because of the circumstances, many men were buried where they fell. However very often these graves were destroyed in subsequent fighting, which does much to explain the large number of unknown burials.

defenders of the wood wrote, 'I never remember having seen so many dead in so small a stretch of ground; in one of the rides they lay five and six deep'.

In that August heat in Delville Wood the first signs of decay showed themselves within four or five hours of the fatal blow, and as so many of the unburied dead had been littering the place for days or even weeks, the air was poisoned with the odour of death. Under such conditions, added to the increasing bombardment, it was possible to hold the wood only by short spells of service in its so-called trenches.

An attempt was made to clear the wood of Germans in the northernmost part on 7 August and the early hours of the 8th, but this failed. This line held by the Germans was known as Inner Trench, and exists (in part) today. The line created by the Borders on August 7 and 8 – or rather repaired and continued – also still exists in part – this is Devil's Trench. They are to be found over to the north eastern part of the wood between Regent Street, Bond Street and the eastern edge of the wood, though the latter extends to the south of Princes Street.

Life in the trenches here had become a terrifying drudge of deadly familiarity – a mixed bunch of words, but disaster lurked around every bush, but men were too exhausted to live their lives on a perpetual 'high'. The line was still not everywhere continuous, and so sounds from all around could presage danger.

Day and night the enemy's fire was unceasing – sniping in the bush at the front, shells of various calibres coming from three directions and including plenty of gas shells, and frequent pelting with machine-gun fire, direct from the enemy's nearer trenches, and indirect fire from longer ranges descending in streams of bullets. The patient endurance with which the men held on is all the more to their credit, because for many of the newcomers it was their first experience of being under fire.

The Brigadier-General commanding 52 Brigade made notes of his first impressions when his Brigade relieved the 51st on the night of 10 August.

Conditions in Delville Wood were appalling. It was full of gas and corpses; no regular line could be discerned, and the men fought in small groups, mostly in shell holes hastily improvised into fire trenches; communications both lateral and from front to rear were exceedingly difficult, dangerous and barely possible.

By the morning of 13 August, the 17th Division was out of Delville Wood for good, relieved by the 14th. Its losses came to over 6,500,

With the Germans at long last removed from Delville Wood, the British set about consolidating their hard won gain.

making it a worse experience than their time before Fricourt and Contalmaison. Thus was the slogging match of the later days of the Somme battle.

9/KRRC

The concluding account in the selections made for the activities of the British in and around Longueval and Delville Wood relates to 9/KRRC, part of 42 Brigade, 14th (Light) Division.

On 18 August the Division had attacked eastwards out of Delville Wood towards Ginchy, and had taken Hop Alley. On 24 August the Battalion was to take part in a larger attack, the job of 9/KRRC being to clear Delville Wood to the north east.

At 3.45 pm on the 24th a bombardment of our heavy artillery started, which fire was replied to by the Germans. At 5.45 pm C and D Companies advanced to the attack, and at the same time A Company moved from the support trench (Devil's Help) and reformed in Devil's Trench, ready to advance. The distance from Devil's Trench to the first objective varied from 250 to 300 yards. The ground was pitted with innumerable shell holes, and obstructed with the debris of fallen trees, necessitating a slow advance. Immediately the barrage lifted, and our assaulting troops climbed over the parapet, the enemy's artillery fire became intense, and machine-gun and rifle fire was opened on them, causing many casualties. All the officers of both C and D Companies were either killed or wounded. The men were rallied and led on by the NCOs.

126

MONT STATION GUILLEMONT RD CEMETERY

TRONES WOOD BERNAFAY WOOD

MEMORIAL

9 / KRRC

EDGE TRENCH

Beyond Edge Trench was Inner Trench, the last outposts of the German Army in Delville Wood .

On the right of Edge Trench the enemy's wire remained to form a considerable obstacle, and the remains of C Company were unable to gain an entry into the trench. The Company Lewis guns, both of C and D Companies, were brought into action close to the German trench and, for a time, until the teams were killed, fired with effect on the enemy.

At 5.45 pm A Company advanced from Devil's Help, forming

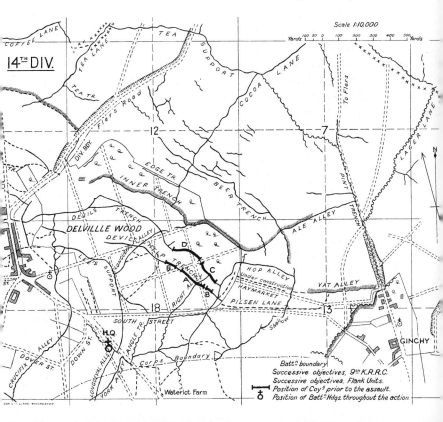

the third wave of the assault, maintaining its direction and formation splendidly. On our right the attack by 8/KRRC from Hop Alley was making no headway, and a party of the Battalion Bombers was ordered to advance towards the junction of Ale and Hop Alley, which they found to be held by two men of 8/KRRC. They were ordered to hold this point at all costs. They established a barricade, from which they bombed the enemy, and held on there until relieved on the morning of the 25th.

At an early stage of the battle every officer of the assaulting companies had become casualties and at 7 pm the officer commanding B Company, in reserve, was mortally wounded. The attack was now entirely held up by the wire, machine-gun and rifle fire – particularly from an enemy strong point situated in Edge Trench, which was found afterwards not to have been seriously damaged by shell fire. Men of A Company managed to enter the enemy's trench and made many prisoners. This trench (Inner Trench) and the dugouts in it were found to contain a *considerable number of German dead.*

One company of 9/RB came up as reinforcements, and early the next morning, at 2 am, bombing attacks were organised. These attacks were carried out, and the enemy's trenches were found to be almost entirely evacuated. As a result of the operations, our objective – the clearing of Delville Wood – with the exception of a small post, was entirely successful. 160 prisoners were captured, including nine officers and some machine-guns.

This really was almost the end of the fighting in Delville Wood, though that 'small post' and Edge trench were to give problems over the next ten days or so.

1. Everard Wyrall, *The 17th (S) Battalion Royal Fusiliers 1914-1919*. Methuen, 1930.
2. Extracts for this section have been taken from A Hilliard Atkinson, *History of the 17th (Northern) Division*. Robert Maclehose & Co Ltd (Glasgow) 1929.

Chapter Seven

CAR TOUR

The duration of the Car Tour can be anything from one and a half hours to three hours, depending on whether the driver stops at the various vantage points or places of interest, and how long is spent in, for example, the cemeteries.

The map used is a trench map: there are disadvantages in doing this, as some of the tracks marked have disappeared and others have been added since the war, but on balance I think it is of assistance to the tourer, putting the ground firmly in the context of 1916.

Start Point: Visitors' Centre Car Park, Delville Wood.

Head towards Longueval. The two German field guns that provided cover for the strong point that held out so stubbornly on 14 July were on the right hand side, in the south west edge of the wood. At the T junction turn left, towards Guillemont. This road was known as High Holborn during the war; to its immediate south ran a track known as Fleet Street, but this no longer exists. The cemetery, at the left hand junction of the road, did not exist before 1914 – it was originally near the church in the village on the west side of the road. Opposite is a rather ramshackle building which used to be the village hall. Running south from it was Down Street **(1)**, which eventually met up with

The numbers relate to the ones in the text. Since the aerial photograph was taken, both Down and Dover Street have been ploughed over.

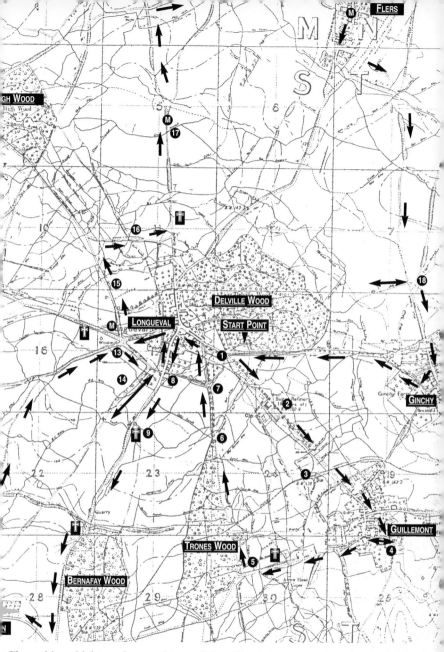

Cheapside, which ran due south out of the village.

Proceed down High Holborn. The German defence line ran in the field immediately adjacent to the road on the right hand side. After about five hundred yards there are some old houses and a great

This view looking towards Guillemont and Trones Wood shows the importance of Delville Wood to both sides in the attack on Guillemont and the developing battle to the south.

expanse of wasteland and derelict buildings. Waterlot Farm **(2)** was rebuilt as a sugar refinery after the war, but had been derelict for many years before the great bulk of the building was demolished a few years ago, thereby removing an eye-sore, but also quite a handy battlefield landmark. The German defence line swept around the west of the building. Six hundred yards or so beyond the farm was Guillemont Station **(3)**, tucked away on the right close to the modern granary tower. The restored station building was only demolished a few years ago. The line running up to the sugar refinery was a branch line from here, but it went beyond the refinery into Longueval itself, presumably offering some form of passenger provision.

Drive through Guillemont, already covered in this series in Mike Stedman's book, *Guillemont*. Pass the church and note the 16th (Irish) Divisional memorial in front of it. The main road sweeps around to the right, but it is worth a small diversion to turn left at this point, and after a couple of hundred yards, on the right, in a small orchard, will be found the entrances to a substantial German dugout system **(4)**. This is on private ground and there is no access to the public.

Turn around and return to the D64, driving past Guillemont Road Cemetery. It might be worthwhile to get out here and look at the views across to Delville Wood, bearing in mind that the Germans were in control of this part of the front for almost all of the time that is under discussion in this book.

A large wood is to be seen to your right front. At the beginning of this wood (Trones) turn right **(5)**. This road takes you along the eastern

View from Guillemont Road Cemetery across to Delville Wood.

side of Trones Wood, which was captured by 18th Division. At the apex of the wood **(6)** the road was known from here to Longueval (and the track coming down its west side) as Cheapside. In later maps Cheapside was also indicated as branching north eastwards some five hundred yards before entering Longueval. There was a communication trench, in part dug by 9/Seaforths, that ran from this point across to Pall Mall, in a north westerly direction, called Folly Trench. Running off in a north easterly direction, which eventually worked its way into Delville Wood was Longueval Alley. About four hundred yards towards Longueval the road begins to flatten out a bit **(7)**; Dover Street ran off to the west (now gone) and Down Street to the north east (also gone). It is possible to make out the line of the latter by spotting the crucifix of the civil cemetery and the building which used to be the village hall. During the war there was a small orchard here. Near where Dover Street joined this road the ground rose to an embankment, and many battalions had their Headquarters tucked in to its southern side. After another two hundred yards Cheapside crosses the site of the railway line and beyond it, immediately to the right of the road and to

the north of the railway line, was the trench that was used by the Highland Brigade to launch counter attacks against the Germans advancing from Delville Wood as the battle progressed. It was near here, too, that the German strong point was that held up the advance of the Highland Brigade on 14 July.

Cheapside now comes on to one of the main village streets, the Peronne Road. Turn left here, and in the main square turn left again. This road was known as Pall Mall. Just as one is leaving the south of the village, on the left hand side between buildings there is a track/road **(8)**. Often there is a bus, used for school runs, parked

Dover Street.

there. This is all that is left of Dover Street. It is possible to walk to the end of what now remains of this road, and peer across the field. Note that it is impossible to see Cheapside, over to the east. The Germans considered Cheapside to be the chief British means of entering Longueval, not least because it was rather more sunken then than it is

Longueval Road Cemetery looking towards Bernafay Wood and Mountauban.

today, and provided a reasonably covered approach.

A few hundred yards out of the village, just before the downward descent begins, Longueval Road Cemetery **(9)** will be found on the left. There is a separate section for a number of cemeteries and memorials, which gives more details. Martin and Mary Middlebrook report in their *Somme Battlefields* that Julius Caesar had important business here with one of his Legions some 1,950 years before the events described in this book. Whilst at the cemetery take the chance to look around the whole sweep of the battlefield area to the east, south and towards the west. It strikes home how considerable was the achievement of British arms on 14 July in capturing this area at all.

Proceed past Bernafay Wood Cemetery (on your right) and the wood of that name on your left (and sparing a thought for the pioneers of the 9th Division busily repairing the road over which you are travelling). At the cross roads, take the right turn into Montauban, noting how the ground drops away both to your left and right as you drive towards the village.

At the first crossroads at the western edge of the village you will turn right. On your left is a memorial to the Liverpool and Manchester Pals, dedicated in 1994. More about Montauban may be read in the book of that name by Graham Maddocks, a leading light in the committee that erected this memorial.

Proceed along this road until the ground starts to fall away into Caterpillar Valley and a track is to be seen on your right **(10)**. This track was the brigade boundary for the 14 July attack. It is possible to walk along this all the way to Longueval, although at places it is very difficult and it is necessary to walk along the field line. Continue about a hundred yards and stop **(11)**. If you scramble up the embankment on the right hand side you are close to Triangle Point, part of the German defences on 1 July and used by the British afterwards. Just beyond it, and running along the north side of Montauban, was Montauban Alley, which wended its way on to Pall Mall and into the northernmost part of Bernafay Wood. Good views may also be had from here across to Longueval.

Proceed to the bottom of the valley, and on the right hand side, set back from the road, will be found Quarry Cemetery **(12)**. This area was used as a rallying area for the German defenders of Montauban on 1 July, and the British made extensive use of it as well during their continuing attacks. On 14 July it marked the left flank of the 9th (Scottish) Division. Turn right at the cemetery along a metalled track,

View from southern edge of Longueval.

TRONES WOOD

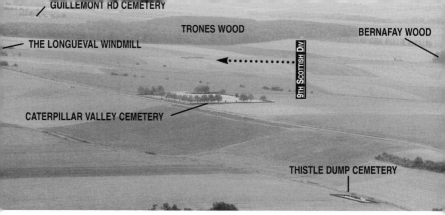

The Longueval windmill, with labels: GUILLEMONT RD CEMETERY, THE LONGUEVAL WINDMILL, TRONES WOOD, 9TH SCOTTISH DIV, BERNAFAY WOOD, CATERPILLAR VALLEY CEMETERY, THISTLE DUMP CEMETERY.

which continued to act as the left flank of the Division. At the road junction at the top, stop **(13)**.

Get out of the car and mount the embankment on your left, near some trees. Looking north west you can see the great mass of High Wood. Directly north, on the other side of the road, is the memorial cross to the 12/Gloucesters. To the west a few hundred yards down the road, is Caterpillar Valley cemetery, one of the largest on the Somme. It is a concentration cemetery, and commands excellent views across Caterpillar Valley from its rear. The 9th Division captured the ground on which it stands, the extreme left of the attack, but a further description may be found in the forthcoming High Wood in this series.

In the area where you are standing there were two windmills, but by 1914 there was only the one.

Turn right, along what was known as Sloane Street; many of the troops coming up to the front were able to find shelter in here from German artillery. After a couple of hundred yards, take the metalled track to the right **(14)**. It might be best to park here and walk a few hundred yards down it, as it is impractical to turn the car around further down. There was an orchard on your left and the line was about fifty yards down here. Proceed until you can see right down Caterpillar Valley, across to Montauban and down to the Quarry Cemetery.

Return to the car (or reverse) and continue along

Longueval windmills.

Labels: ONGUEVAL RD CEMETERY, BERNAFAY WOOD, MONTAUBAN TO LONGUEVAL TRACK, MONTAUBAN, German Front Line 14 July

A pre-war photograph of the Rue de Peronne, which leads to Delville Wood from the square.

Sloane Street, either going down the small street on your left or proceeding to Pall Mall and turning left there. The houses along here all had to be cleared of German snipers and machine-guns, and a number were converted into British strongpoints. At the square, turn left. This road, towards the two Bazentins, was known as Clarges Street and was the scene of the most bitter fighting. The main British trench system ran to the north of it for some while, and there were other systems to the immediate south. At the crossroads where the 12/Gloucesters cross is, turn right, signposted Martinpuich. Drive slowly down the road, looking to your right. After about two hundred yards, on your right, was the site of Duke Street, discussed further in the First Walk. In the fields on this side of the road the most terrific struggles took place. There is a cross roads **(15)** a few hundred yards on – or rather a track crosses the metalled road. This did not exist in 1914; to the left it goes towards Thistle Dump Cemetery and on the right it goes through to a village dump. It is possible to walk a little way along here. To the south was where 76 Brigade came charging in from the west in the early hours of 18 July, and it was not far from this location that one of the great heroes of the war Major Billy Congreve, VC DSO MC, was killed.

Terry Norman, who died tragically young, produced a first rate edition of Congreve's diary; *Armageddon Road, A VC's diary 1914 – 1916* was printed in 1982 by William Kimber.

Congreve was the Brigade Major and came up to see what had gone wrong with the early morning attack and to try and clarify the situation. He crossed over Pont Street (the road to High Wood and Martinpuich) and went to the line that 2/Suffolks was consolidating, Duke Street. This was about two hundred yards to the south of the track on which you are standing. The western side of Duke Street is now incorporated in a field, but it is possible to see part of its outline from your location and also from Piccadilly (see Walking Tour 1). Congreve

General Sir Walter Congreve, VC.

made various notes about the position, but was shot, at about 11 am, by a sniper as he talked to a group of men who were digging a sap.

Congreve's father, the Corps Commander, had won his VC at Colenso in 1899, in part for attempting to save the life of Lieutenant FS Roberts, himself the son of a VC, Lord Roberts. The Congreves were one of three cases in which father and son both won the VC.

Major Congreve's citation reads,

For most conspicuous bravery during a period of fourteen days preceding his death in action (6 – 20 July). This officer constantly performed acts of gallantry and showed the greatest devotion to duty, and by his personal example inspired all those around him with confidence at critical periods of the operations. During preliminary preparations for the attack he carried out personal reconnaisances of the enemy lines, taking out parties of officers and non-commissioned officers for over 1,000 yards in front of our lines [This would have been prior to the dawn attack of 14 July] *in order to acquaint them with the ground. All these preparations were made under fire.*

Later, by night, Major Congreve conducted a battalion to its position of employment, afterwards returning to it to ascertain the situation after an assault. He established himself in an exposed forward position from whence he successfully observed the enemy, and gave orders necessary to drive them from their position. Two days later, when Brigade Headquarters were heavily shelled and many casualties resulted, he went out and assisted the medical officer to remove the wounded to places of safety, although he himself was severely suffering from gas and other shell effects. He again on a subsequent occasion showed supreme courage in tending wounded under heavy shell fire.

137

> *He finally returned to the front line to ascertain the situation after an unsuccessful attack, and whilst in the act of writing his report was shot and killed instantly.*

Congreve, a dynamic twenty-five year-old, was buried the next day at Corbie. Duty meant that his father had first to attend a conference with Rawlinson at Fourth Army Headquarters, but he was then able to see his son in the mortuary. He

> *was struck by his beauty and strength of face. I felt inspired by his look and know that he is 'helping' me, as he used to say, and that he always will do so. I never felt so proud of him as I did when I said goodbye to him.*
>
> *A lot of flowers were sent by kind people, amongst them wild mallows from the fighting line by some of the men. These I had put into the grave; and a huge wreath tied with the tricolour ribband from General Balfourier. I myself put in his hand a posey of poppies, cornflowers and daisies ... and with a kiss I left him.*

Congreve had married several weeks earlier, in June 1916, and a daughter was born eight months or so after his death. His widow went on to marry, in December 1919, a great soldier friend of Billy's, William Fraser, DSO MC, whose own letters and diaries were published in 1990, edited by his son, General Sir David Fraser.

Return to your car, and as the road begins to flatten out on the north side of the valley, turn right. After about four hundred yards, on your left, a track emerges **(16)**. Along this ran Wood Lane, part of the German defences of High Wood and Longueval. Proceed along the road until you can see clearly down into Longueval and over the embankment. In the dip you will see the football ground of Longueval FC, and there is a track running down from this road which wends its way past the football ground and up into Longueval, coming out at Clarges Street. This track was the infamous Piccadilly, and to the left of the track, from approximately beyond the football field (ie to its south), right up to Clarges Street, were the infamous orchards. Just to the south of the road on which your car is standing was Orchard Trench, which the Manchesters, Duke of Wellingtons and Northumberland Fusiliers attacked in vain in the early days of August. Duke Street was just beyond the expanse of water some three hundred yards beyond the football field.

At the road junction, where there stands a Calvary, turn left. This road was called North Street and used to be a cul de sac until a recent *remembrement* opened up the track to Flers. Drive up to the New

A view of Delville Wood and Longueval from the New Zealand Memorial.

DELVILLE WOOD

Zealand Memorial (discussed in forthcoming titles) and stop **(17)**. Get out of your car and look towards Delville Wood and appreciate the contour upon which it sits. To the east of the wood is where the 163rd Regiment prepared for its various attacks against the British and South Africans in the wood. The west edge of the wood may be observed, and the north west edge is the approximate site of Point 140. It is also possible to make out the Flers road, which disappears into dead ground, and along which many of the German troops came to reinforce their compatriots. It also provides good views to the south and across to Caterpillar Valley cemetery and High Wood to the west.

Drive around the back of the memorial, follow the good quality track down into the valley and turn right into Flers. Follow this road until you arrive at what is obviously the main road. To the left it goes to Guedecourt and Ligny-Thilloy and ultimately Bapaume. Turn right, driving through the village, but noting the splendid memorial to the 41st Division, a Tommy in full fighting order. A duplicate is to be found just outside Chancery Lane tube station, on High Holborn in London.

The road south swings sharply to the right and then left and it was just beyond this, on the right, that the Germans had a regimental Headquarters at the beginning of the fighting at Delville Wood. It had to be moved out to the Ginchy road after it was destroyed by shell fire. Just as the built up village comes to an end there is a small turning to the left, signposted to Ginchy. Take this road. The Headquarters was relocated in the sunken road along here.

On the Flers side of the civilian cemetery there is a new track **(18)** that leads towards the eastern edge of Delville Wood. About fifty yards north of it was Ale Alley, which crossed this track where it makes a sharp turn; at this point, about a hundred yards to the south, was Hop Alley. It is difficult to turn around on this track, and it peters out, so be prepared to reverse a considerable distance.

Return to the main road and drive into Ginchy, turning right towards Guillemont and almost immediately right again towards Longueval. Note the views across to the south west and the rising ground on your right. The edge of Delville Wood marks the scene of bitter fighting through the second half of July and all of August.

Angle Trench used to run from the approximate site of the entrance to the cemetery and the Memorial, and went in a south westerly direction where it connected with High Holborn and Longueval Alley, about two hundred yards north west of Waterlot Farm.

Return to the Visitors' Centre car park.

LONGUEVAL

ORCHARD TRENCH

WALKING TOURS

There are two walking tours, each with their own map.

Tour One: this should take One Hour to an Hour and a Half.

Park the car near the church **(1)** in Longueval. During the war the church was on the south side of the road, a few metres back towards Longueval. It is commonly believed locally that there was a tunnel running from the crypt of the old church through Delville Wood, which emerged at a sunken part of the Flers road at the north west edge of the wood. Next door to the church was the Presbytery. On the north side was the cemetery, now a patch of green. One pre-war grave stone remains, laid flat in the ground. Near to this was the Hospice, a convent for the elderly. Next to the green bottle bank, somewhat incongruously, is a heavy British trench mortar. Behind the church, and towards Delville Wood, was the site of the chateau, more or less at the end of Princes Street. The site of this building is more easily discerned from the Delville Wood side.

It is in this area that the famous charge at Longueval took place on the evening of 18 July, soon after 6 pm. Members of the Black Watch, Seaforths and anyone else available were lined up in a trench **(A)** which ran south of the Peronne road, with its left flank on Cheapside and its right on Down Street,

G. T..... édit. à Albert

The Chateau is through the arch at the end of the road; the modern church now stands approximately where the arch is now. The presbytery was to the right front of the church.

just behind the dilapidated building which was the Village Hall. This building is more or less opposite the civil cemetery. This trench was just to the north of the railway line that ran into the village. Meanwhile the Camerons were alerted to join in from their positions in Buchanan Street. The men in the trench set off half left towards the village square, the Camerons joining on their flank and ran straight into the Germans coming out of the south west edge of Delville Wood. The Germans decided that discretion was the better part of valour, and headed back for the shelter of the broken forest, chased by the Highlanders.

Walk down the street (this continuation of the main central ride was also known as Princes Street) towards the main square. On the right was the town pond, now tarmaced over. The café on the right looks

No longer a place for ladies' fashions, the replacement building is a bar.

LONGUEVAL. - LA MAIRIE
ET L'ECOLE DES GARÇONS - P. D.

The town hall looks remarka[bly]
similiar to its pre-war predeces[sor]
– though the present generation[of]
schoolboy does not wear a dress[.]
A lot of the very heavy str[eet]
fighting took place on this side [of]
the road.

Rather similar buildings today house a
bar (but not a restaurant) and a petrol
station – one of the few on the battlefield.

very similar to a similar pre-war establishment. Drinks (but not food) may be purchased both there and one on the opposite side of the square, on Pall Mall. For much of the fighting the square was barricaded, as was North Street, the road to Flers. Take the road towards Bazentin, Clarges Street, the scene of heavy fighting for much of the time on late July. At a waste disposal point turn right: this is Piccadilly **(2)**. The British more or less managed to hold the ground to the left, the Germans were in the orchards and buildings on the right. Follow this quite muddy track until there is a turning on the right – this is the remaining part of the track that was Duke Street. Its outline may be seen on the field in the left, which is usually easily accessible, but this is private property and should be respected as such.

This was the line to which men of the 17th(Northern) Division came in August. Their objective on 4 August was the German trench (Orchard Trench **3**) that ran just in front of the cross road that connects Pont Street with North Street. Turn right here until you reach the Calvary **(4)** and look carefully at the view that the Germans had over Longueval and the wood. Orchard Trench continued to run from just south of this position more or less directly

Junction of Piccadilly and Duke Street; the track to the left leads to North Street. The extension of Duke Street eastwards is discernible but is on private land.

NEW ZEALAND MEMORIAL

Top: a view of Piccadilly at the north end.

Below: Piccadilly at the village end.

It is hard to imagine the mayhem that took place here in July 1916. Longueval has not expanded much beyond its old boundaries.

eastwards, across the Flers road and into Delville Wood.

Turn right and proceed south down North Street (!) During the war there was a small orchard in the gap between the two roads, and it was in here that the British thought there was a Post **(e)** when the 17th Division took over the sector. There was not.

Walk up North Street towards the centre of Longueval. There was heavy street fighting in these houses on both sides of the road in the days when the 9th (Scottish) Division were trying to wrest Longueval and Delville Wood from German hands. The situation was extraordinarily confusing for everyone – for the British, the South Africans and the Germans; for the commanders and for the soldiers; for the Infantry and the Artillery.

Return to your car and drive to the Visitors' Centre at Delville Wood.

The French government was keen to encourage the refugees to return to their villages as soon as possible. Below is Longueval's temporary church.

TOUR 2. DELVILLE WOOD

Note that Prince's Street is usually written Princes Street in all the records and history of the time, and I have stayed with that usage.

This tour can take anything up to three hours or more, depending how long one wants to spend exploring the wood; at least two hours should be allowed for a decent inspection.

Although the battle was in July and August, it is in March that one can see most because the foliage will have died away and the branches are clear.

It is one of the unfortunate aspects about most visitors who come to Delville Wood that they fail to visit the most significant parts of the wood. This is not to underplay the importance of the command position in Buchanan Street, but much of the most vicious fighting took place along

The Visitors' Centre and car park at Delville Wood.

Princes Street and the ground to its immediate north and south; whilst very few venture to the perimeter to the north west, the north east and the east, where so many gallant deeds were done.

Commence this tour by walking to the cemetery **(A)**. Angle Trench ran through it, entering the park more of less where the entrance to the Memorial is, and ten to the southern edge of Campbell Street and King Street, between which is the new access road to the museum for emergency vehicles.

It is probably best to make your way over to the west of the wood, finding Buchanan Street **(B)** some yards in from the west edge of the wood. Walk along this until you come to a stone which states that it marks the site of the South African battle Headquarters. Follow the

Delville Wood Cemetery shortly after it was finally established, but the wood shows only the earliest signs of recovering.

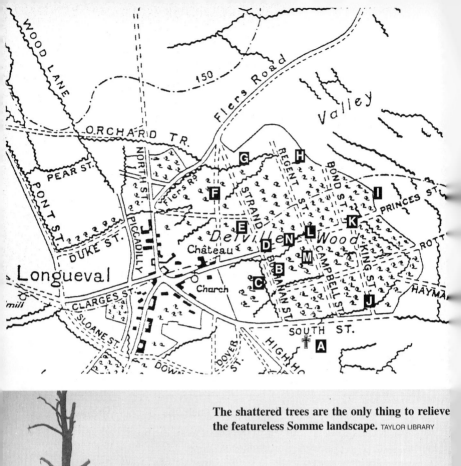

The shattered trees are the only thing to relieve the featureless Somme landscape. TAYLOR LIBRARY

The point at which the South Africans entered the wood and from which the Camerons launched their charge.

path behind it, noting the trench line, which leads out to the south western edge of the wood, where another marker **(C)** indicates that this is the point at which the South Africans entered the wood for the first time. It is also the area where the Camerons set off for their charge in the evening of 18 July. The Cameron Highlanders was the only regiment that carried the battle honour **Delville Wood** on their Colours.

Follow the track to the right (ie north) and then follow the perimeter path all the way around. After a while the great central ride, Princes Street, will be seen **(D)**. Note that these rides are far, far wider than they were in 1914 – anywhere up to four times wider. Look towards the village and the church is seen quite clearly. The raised ground in between you and the church marks the site of the chateau and its various outbuildings. It was

A view of the Chateau and its outbuildings from the Delville Wood end. It was used by the Germans as a headquarters.

never rebuilt after the war.

Continue along the perimeter track, following it around as it swings to the right **(E)**. The raised ground in the field beyond is also part of the chateau complex. As the track comes around to the north again you are in the part of the wood **(F)** that the Germans were able to hang on to most easily, with their position reasonably secure in the northern part of Longueval itself. It is possible to get good views from here **(G)** up to the New Zealand Memorial and High Wood beyond – his was ground under clear German observation. Continue to walk around the whole perimeter – you should be getting a clear feel of the concave hill on which the wood sat. For a short time the wood marches alongside the Flers Road, and this was often used by the Germans as an entry point into the wood, as was the stretch beyond it, until the perimeter path turns sharply south west. Continue to look out to the north **(H)** and the east and at the folding nature of the ground of Flers and how the Church spire at Ginchy is hidden from view for several hundred yards. The Germans could approach the wood relatively easily, but were of course very vulnerable when it came to the last few hundred yards. Edge Trench ran almost the whole length of this north eastern and eastern edge of the wood **(I)**, and it was along here that the Germans held on to the bitter end in the great struggle, not really being seen off until September.

Walk up King Street **(J)** until you get to the central ride, Princes Street **(K)**. En route you will notice at least one reasonably cleared trench line along which one may walk, and this is probably Devil's Support. Turn left at Princes Street and then go down Bond Street. Trench lines can be seen here, one of which is possibly Devil's Trench,

The ground beyond the fence to the left is where the Chateau buildings once stood.

A view from the west side of the wood looking towards the village. It was this area which was held most tenaciously by the Germans.

a British trench, and the other Inner Trench, a German trench. These have been identified as belonging to the respective nationalities by the equipment that was removed when they were cleared. Also to be found is the bed of an old railway line.

Return to Princes Street **(L)** and proceed towards the Memorial.

On the morning of 20 July 10/Royal Welsh Fusiliers took part in the attack of 76 Brigade, and in the course of it won two VCs. Standing on Princes Street is as good as any way to read of what happened. The Regimental History records the bare details.

The guides were met [in the early hours of 20 July] *at the south west corner of the wood, and they led the battalion up the side of Buchanan Street held by the South Africans. At this point our troubles began. Although, apparently, we were nowhere near Princes Street, we were met by a considerable amount of machine-gun fire: Verey* [sic] *lights went up a short distance to our front, and the Germans were heard shouting all over the wood. It was maintained by the guide that we were close to Princes Street, but this could not be the case as we had advanced only 150 yards from the south edge of the wood. The only possible course seemed to be to deploy, so a compass bearing was taken and a star selected due east for the leader of the deployment to march on.*

The original intention was that three companies should deploy behind the line Princes Street, each on a 200-yards frontage; B on the right, D in the centre and C on the left, with A in reserve.

Officers from each company were then to go forward to mark the limit of the advance on the flanks and at the centre; their men would

The detritus of war – an artillery piece, a limber and a scattering of shells litter the streets of Longueval

One of the smaller paths in Delville Wood; these were often trenches or old railway beds.

then advance, and on reaching their position would turn left and thus sweep the wood. In fact the Germans attacked B Company on the right, shortly after they started to deploy. They were beaten off, but the attack was repeated again after the Company had moved on another two hundred yards. A description of what actually took place in the remnants of the wood, at night, is impossible. However, during the general chaos of fighting enough was discerned to result in the awarding of two Victoria Crosses.

Between these two German attacks, Corporal Joseph Davies, with eight men, became separated from his Company (D). Before he could rejoin them the second German attack was made, and he, with his eight men, was surrounded. He took cover in a shell hole, and by throwing bombs and opening rapid fire routed them. Not content with this, he followed them up in their retreat, and bayoneted several of them. Corporal Davies set a magnificent example of pluck and determination. The credit of repulsing the German second attack was, therefore, entirely Corporal Davies's.

Chaos was caused by fire being opened on 10/Royal Welsh Fusiliers by a neighbouring battalion, which claimed to be ignorant of the dawn attack. Casualties were heavy, but order was restored. At last the attack resumed at 3.45 am.

Naturally the wood was by this time in a turmoil, and C Company, on the left, was met by machine-gun fire and bombs, and checked. The Company Commander, however, rallied his men and led them forward level with the other companies. But the line was broken up, officer casualties, and among the men, were severe, and with the resultant lack of co-operation it became impossible for the advance to continue. The line had to be withdrawn. Many parties, however, could not get back, or never received the order, and lay out all day, engaged in sniping duels with the enemy.

Private Albert Hill had, dashed forward, when the order to charge was given, and meeting two of the enemy suddenly, bayoneted them both. He was sent later

Princes Street looking east in the early 20s. Almost uniform usage in the war spelt it Princes Street, but it should be Prince's.

by his platoon sergeant to get into touch with his company, and, finding himself cut off and almost surrounded by the enemy, attacked them with bombs, killing and wounding many, and scattering the remainder. He then joined a sergeant of his company and helped him to fight the way back to the lines. When he got back, hearing that his company officer and a scout were lying out wounded, he went out and assisted to bring in the wounded officer, two other men bringing in the scout. Finally, he himself captured and brought in as prisoners two of the enemy. His conduct throughout was magnificent.

Corporal Davies was 27 when he performed his deed of valour; wounded at Delville Wood, he eventually was deemed to be unfit for active duty, being discharged finally in December 1918 as a Sergeant. He died in 1976. Private A Hill was just over 21 when he fought at Delville Wood. After the war he emigrated to the USA, and died there in 1971.

The actions above took place in the ground just to the north of Princes Street and towards the western side of the wood. Ponder what you have read in the preceding pages about went on along here, just to the north and south, in the sultry days of July and August 1916: days of unimaginable hell and chaos. The contrast with today's sylvan calm is quite astounding.

Take this opportunity to visit the museum (see cemeteries and memorials section). To the rear and west of the memorial, on the north side of Princes Street, will be found a hornbeam and an explanatory plaque – the sole surviving living thing that was at Delville Wood on 14 July 1916.

Walk back along the great approach aisle and return to the Visitors' Centre. Note that the lawn and flower bed edgings around the Curator's house are made up of unfused shells.

The heaviest fighting in Delville Wood took place to the right of the museum, particularly from Regent Street across to North Street in Longueval.

Chapter Eight

CEMETERIES AND MEMORIALS

Cemeteries

Although there are other cemeteries in the area covered by this book, they have either been included in other books in this series or will appear in further publications.

1. Longueval Road Cemetery
2. Bernafay Wood British Cemetery
3. Quarry Cemetery
4. Caterpillar Valley Cemetery
5. Delville Wood Military Cemetery.

1. Longueval Road Cemetery

The cemetery was begun in September 1916, as for so many cemeteries, because it was near a Dressing Station known as Longueval Alley or Longueval Water Point, the latter for obvious reasons. The communication trench of that name, which ran from Trônes Wood up into Delville Wood, ran close by. The track running to the east side of Bernafay Wood was also there at the time of the war.

As is usually the case, except where numbers of graves have been concentrated after the war, rarely are casualties from the immediate area of the fighting to be found. This is because many of these who died of wounds did so in Dressing Stations further back, or at CCS or Base Hospitals further back again. Those who were killed at the time were often buried (if possible) on the spot, and their graves were lost in the fighting which, as is known for here at Longueval, was exceptionally long and vicious.

At the time of the Armistice there were 171 buried here, with 49 others being brought in between 1923 and 1924. The cemetery ceased to be used in

Longueval Cemetery still in the process of creation in the early post war period.

January 1917, but was reopened during the very last phase of the fighting on the Somme, in August and September 1918.

Because of its high position it is possible to see over a great extent of ground to the south of Longueval.

One entry in the register particularly caught my eye. Corporal Wilfred Dawson (C.8) was killed, aged 34, whilst serving in 190 Brigade Royal Field Artillery on 26 September 1916. Before the war he was the Headmaster of Carshalton School in Surrey. He must have been a very young (and therefore, presumably, a very promising) headteacher; yet he was only a corporal. In Row D.3 is buried Soldier R Pusch of the German Army, who was killed (probably dying of wounds) on 15 October 1916. Most of the burials in the cemetery are from the fighting to the north of Flers, in the latter half of September 1916 and the final weeks of the battle. It is likely that most of the 48 unknown out of the 223 burials in the cemetery were those brought in well after the war ended. In those days of the war the ID disc was made of leather, and would have disintegrated by the early 1920s. A recent body discovered near the lip of the Lochnagar Crater at La Boisselle (in November 1998) was identified by his razor, on which was inscribed his name, regiment and number.

2. Bernafay Wood Cemetery.

This is a deceptively large cemetery, due to the contours of the ground. There are 945 buried here, of whom rather more than forty percent are unknown. The Willow stream meandered its way along the bottom (northern) edge of the cemetery, but it has now ceased to exist.

One other cemetery was incorporated into this one: **Bernafay Wood North Cemetery** was on the other side of the road and just to the north of the wood; it was badly damaged during various phases of the fighting on the Somme, that did not end here until late August 1916. The bodies were brought into Bernafay Wood when the war ended it was the site of an ADS and used from July to October 1916.

Bernafay Wood Cemetery was also the site of an ADS, and burials were started here in August 1916. At the armistice there were 284 and then 638 were concentrated to it. Those concentrated provided the bulk of those with no known grave. Besides those from Bernafay Wood North Cemetery, these came from the eastern side of Bernafay Wood (ie a lot would have been involved in the fighting for Trônes Wood) and there appear to be none who were involved in the fighting for Longueval and Delville Wood after 13 July 1916.

3. Quarry Cemetery, Montauban.

It is a shame that the ground around Quarry Cemtery has become a sort of farmer's dump, because this is one of the most beautifully located cemeteries, to my mind, on this part of the Somme. Nestling right at the base of Caterpillar Valley, there are excellent views along the valley floor, but well hidden from most of the surrounding settlements. There are 741 buried here, 583 of who are known.

At the time of the armistice there were 152 buried here, to be found in Plots

Quarry Cemetery, which is situated in the floor of Caterpillar Valley.

V and VI. The rest were concentrated after the war from the immediate vicinity or from some of the smaller burial grounds. Almost everyone was killed fighting on the Somme in the second half of 1916.

Briqueterie Cemetery No 3 was to the east of the brickworks, south east of Montauban. There were 23 soldiers there, mainly from 1/5 King's Own (Royal Lancaster Regiment). **Caterpillar Valley Cemetery No 2** was at the east end of Caterpillar Wood, several hundred yards away to the west of the present cemetery. It was begun by 2/Suffolks, the battalion which made so little progress in the dawn attack of 20 July, and which Billy Congreve was visiting when he was killed. There were 50 men buried there, and that cemetery remained in use until January 1917. **Green Dump Cemetery** was close to the track along which the tour will take you subsequent to this stop, about three quarters of a mile from Longueval. It contained the graves of 54 soldiers, 11 of whom were from New Zealand, who were killed between August and October 1916. **Quarry Scottish Cemetery** has already been discussed in the main text. 55 men, mainly from 11 and 12/Royal Scots were buried there, all of whom were killed in July 1916.

Lord Ronald Bateman (an interesting Christian name!) was killed at the age of 19 whilst serving with the 22nd Royal Fusiliers. The register notes that he was the youngest of six sons, 'all of whom served'. Second Lieutenant Hugh Brown is recorded as being an engineer, but was killed whilst serving in the infantry 11/Royal Scots.

I was lucky to be visiting Quarry Cemetery on a lovely, sunny, June morning and to have with me Croft's *Three Years with the 9th (Scottish) Division*. It was a wonderfully evocative spot to be reading this book, his descriptions of the fighting here in mid-July 1916, and his poignant descriptions of many of those who ended up in this little cemetery. It will not be to everyone's taste – possible repellent to the spirit of our age; but to my mind I think if reflects far more the atmosphere and morale of that earlier age, no matter what our revisionist historians, steeped in the peculiarly barren philosophical concept of post-modernism, would have us believe.

4. Caterpillar Valley Cemetery

This cemetery will be covered in more detail in a subsequent volume. I include it here purely for personal reasons. Buried in VI E 11 is Lieutenant Colonel William Drysdale, DSO, of 2/Royal Scots, who was killed on 29 September 1916. I mention him because, at the time of his death, he was commanding 7/Leicesters, my grandfather's battalion. In his diary my grandfather noted that he saw a stretcher with a body on it, covered with a blanket. When he pulled the blanket back he saw that it was his commanding officer, with a hole drilled through his head. He had been looking over the top in the Leicesters' new positions around Guedecourt, which they had captured, and been shot by an alert German sniper.

Delville Wood Cemetery

This cemetery was made after the armistice and was the result of the work of Grave Registration units, although a few small cemeteries were concentrated here. Of these, the most proximate was **Lone Ridge Cemetery** which was situated between Delville Wood and Longueval, containing the bodies of 52 men from the 38th (Welsh) Division and the 6th Dragoon Guards, who recaptured the area in August 1918. At the time when the register was prepared there were buried here 5,236 men, including 152 South Afticans. In recent years there have been a few burials of men found in the locality, particularly in Delville Wood. 3,590 of the graves are of unknown soldiers. There is the grave of one VC in the cemetery, Sergeant Gill in IV.C.3, whose exploits are described elsewhere.

The register is usually present in the cupboard provided, but if not there is a copy held both in the Museum and the reception area adjacent to the Visitiors' Car Park. It seems invidious to pick out names from so many, and I would recommend spending the time to walk amongst the serried ranks of headstones, looking at the inscriptions and taking the register with you. There are representatives of all the Dominions present in the cemetery, but no Germans, probably because this was a Concentration cemetery and any found at this stage would have been removed to the limited number of German cemeteries in the vicinity.

IWGC workers preparing Delville Wood Cemetery. These men were ex-soldiers and many of them settled permanently in France or Belgium.

Memorials

1. 12/Gloucesters (Bristol's Own) Memorial Cross
2. South African Memorial, Delville Wood

1. 12/Gloucesters Memorial Cross

12/Gloucesters were part of 95 Brigade, 5th Division. This part of the Somme was their first big battle since landing in France towards the end of November 1915. In late July 1916 they were part of XV Corps. On 29 July at 3.30 pm, after a short bombardment of half an hour, 95 Brigade made a further attack. 12/Gloucesters attacked from the area of the cross and extended the British line northwards some five hundred yards beyond Duke Street. Although this line could not, eventually, be held, it was a notable achievement, and the Battalion chose this site to erect their memorial. The Battalion was not to see the end of the war, as it was disbanded on 19 October 1918, some three weeks before the Armistice.

The original memorial was lost during the Second World War, but was replaced in 1986 thanks to widespread support in the Bristol area and from the local population of Longueval, all largely motivated by Mr Dean Marks. His action is typical of many in the last fifteen years or so, which has ensured the survival or rehabilitation of memorials. There are numerous examples in the immediate area surrounding Longueval, perhaps the most notable of which has been the restoration of the 47th (London) Division memorial on the edge of High Wood.

2. South African Memorial, Delville Wood.

The Memorial originally consisted of the screen, the two shelters on either side and an arch in the middle surmounted by a horse and two figures, representing the two races of the Union. After the Second World War the stone of sacrifice was added as a memorial to those who fell in that conflict; whilst the impressive museum was added very recently. Originally it was intended to purchase the land adjacent to the Flers road, so that the swathe would be right across the wood and the memorial visible from both ends, but it was not to be, and the present arrangement, at least to my mind, seems the more satisfactory.

Unlike all the other national memorials erected by member nations of the Empire, this one does not have names inscribed on the walls. Instead the names of those who were killed in action or died of wounds are written in a book kept in the museum. 229,000 men saw service from the Union of South Africa; 10,000 of these died. Service took the shape of members of the South African Brigade here on the Western Front; of various members of the Labour Corps and those who served in the various campaigns in Africa, mainly in what was German South West Africa, now Namibia.

The museum was constructed in time for the seventieth anniversary of the battle of the Somme, and whatever the political considerations that inspired it, or controversies that surrounded it the present happier situation means that the problems of the present need no longer overshadow what these men of all races achieved and suffered during the war.

The shape of the castle is a replica of the Castle of Good Hope in Capetown. The interior is full of light, coming through beautifully engraved windows. The *voortrekkers'* cross is now in the middle of the interior courtyard. As a counterpoint to the glass are magnificent and evocative bas-reliefs; and there are displays of the various actions in which the South Africans were involved in a number of conflicts up to the Korean War. Further information and booklets may be obtained from the information desk. Access to the museum is free, it is open every day except Monday and French National Holidays and in the winter months; though it is usually open by the middle of February.

FURTHER READING

Ian Uys has written two books on the fighting in Delville Wood and Longueval. The first is the extremely detailed *Delville Wood*, an account of the days spent by the South Aftrican Brigade in the horrific fighting of mid-July. It is an outstanding tribute of the men who fought there, and offers numerous interviews with members of the South African Brigade, a list of men killed in the action, officer casualties and decorations. Although printed as far back as 1983, it is still readily available. Mr Uys followed this volume up with a rather slimmer, stiff backed book, *Longueval*, which gives an account of the German viewpoint of the period up to 23 July. This was published in 1986 and is also readily available.

The South African Brigade had their history written by the very versatile author and statesman, John Buchan. His *South African Forces in the Field* has been reprinted relatively recently, and so no longer commands quite the horrendous prices that it once did in the second hand book market. In 1993 Peter Digby published *Pyramids and Poppies*, which has updated and expanded John Buchan's work, and is profusely illustrated.

There are now a tremendous number of guides to the Somme battlefield. The core guide for well over twenty years now has been Rose Coombs's *Before Endeavours Fade*, and this excellent battlefield vade mecum continues to be regularly updated. Gerald Gliddon first published *When the Barrage Lifts* in 1987, and this topographical survey of the Somme battlefield is enhanced by his frequent references to memoirs and other accounts. Martin and Mary Middlebrook, veteran guides of the battlefields, have written one of the most readable battlefield guides in print, *The Somme Battlefields,* and is most strongly recommended. In this series, Paul Reed has written *Walking the Somme*, designed for the more energetic, a series of walks on the battlefield. The most recent entry to this field has been *Major and Mrs Holt's Battlefield Guide to the Somme*. This book is the product of many years work leading groups around the battlefields, and is enhanced by a clear and most useful map.

INDEX